**Books are to be returned on or before
the last date below.**

54118

Frank Wedekind: Spring Awakening
in a new version by Ted Hughes

Frank Wedekind (1864–1918) was born in Hanover. He became a journalist and later secretary of a circus before forming his own theatrical company and producing and acting in his own plays. *Fruhlings Erwachen* (*Spring Awakening*) was written in 1891 and like all his plays aroused great controversy for its sexual outspokenness. It is perhaps his best known work.

Ted Hughes was born in 1930. He is the author of numerous collections of poems and books for adults and children. His adaptation of Seneca's *Oedipus* was performed at the Old Vic Theatre, London in 1968. In 1971/2 he worked with Peter Brook at his International Centre for Theatre Research in Paris. In 1984 he was appointed Poet Laureate. This version of *Spring Awakening* was commissioned by the Royal Shakespeare Company and first performed in The Pit at the Barbican, London, in August 1995.

FRANK WEDEKIND

Spring Awakening

in a new version
by Ted Hughes

faber and faber
LONDON · BOSTON

First published in 1995
by Faber and Faber Limited
3 Queen Square London WC1N 3AU

Photoset by Parker Typesetting Service, Leicester
Printed in England by Clays Ltd, St Ives plc

All applications for professional and amateur rights should be addressed in
the first instance to Faber and Faber Limited, 3 Queen Square,
London WC1N 3AU

A CIP record for this book
is available from the British Library

ISBN 0-571-17791-3

2 4 6 8 10 9 7 5 3 1

This version of **Spring Awakening** was first performed by the Royal Shakespeare Company at The Pit in the Barbican, London, on 2 August 1995. The cast was as follows:

Wendla Bergman Ellie Beaven
Frau Bergman Ruth Mitchell
Melchior Gabor Andrew Falvey
Otto Sebastian Brennan
Moritz Steifel Barry Farrimond
Georg Daniel Bennet
Ernst Robel Kristopher Milnes
Hans Rilow Oliver Grig
Martha Bessel Elizabeth Cornfield
Thea Polly Findlay
Professor Knockenbruch Simon Cook
Professor Hungergurt Alec Bregonzi
Frau Gabor Sara Mair-Thomas
Ilse Catherine Bailey
Sonnenstich Raymond Bowers
Pastor Kahlbauch Roy Ward
Zungenschlag Raymond Mason
Probst Alec Bregonzi
Herr Steifel Raymond Mason
Herr Gabor David Glover
Rienhold Oliver Grig
Ruprecht Daniel Bennet
Helmuth Kristopher Milnes
Gaston Sebastian Brennan
Dr Prokrustes Raymond Mason

Locksmith Roy Ward
Dr Brausepulver Alec Bregonzi
Ina Bergman Samantha Robson
Masked Gentleman Mike Burnside

Directed by Tim Supple
Designed by Tom Piper
Lighting by Paule Constable
Music arranged and selected by Glyn Perrin

Act One

SCENE ONE

Bergmans' living-room.

Wendla You've made it so long, Mother. It's too long.

Frau Bergman Wendla, you're not a little girl any more, this is your fourteenth birthday.

Wendla I'd rather never be fourteen than have to wear a dress this long.

Frau Bergman It is not too long. What can we do? Every spring you've shot up another two inches. You're a young woman now, Wendla. That little-princess frock is beginning to look ridiculous on you.

Wendla It suits me better than this dreary thing. Oh, Mother, let me go on wearing it. Just this summer. Till my next birthday. This will keep – Look at it, it gives me an awful feeling. It's like a prison sack or something for criminals. My legs would feel trapped in it.

Frau Bergman Ah, Wendla, if only I could keep you exactly as you are now. At your age most girls are such gangly, awkward creatures, but you're exactly the opposite. When they're all full-grown, what will you be like, I wonder?

Wendla Maybe I shan't be here.

Frau Bergman My darling child, where do you get such ideas?

Wendla Oh, Mother, don't be upset, I'm sorry.

Frau Bergman My precious little darling.

Wendla But I do sometimes think about it. Sometimes at night when I can't sleep. Thoughts like that just come. They don't make me sad at all. And they do make me sleep. Is it bad to think those thoughts, Mother? Is it sinful?

Frau Bergman Here you are – go and hang it in the wardrobe. Wear your little-princess frock if that's what you want. Perhaps I can tack a bit of flounce round the hem some time.

Wendla Please no, not that. I'd rather be twenty right now.

Frau Bergman I don't want you to catch a chill, Wendla. That little dress used to be long enough but –

Wendla Mother, it's nearly summer. You don't catch diphtheria in your knees. You're such a worrier. Girls my age don't get frostbite – least of all in the legs. Would you prefer me too hot? How if I were too hot? What if your precious little darling cut off the sleeves altogether, right up to the armpits. What if I came home one night without shoes or stockings or knickers? When I wear that prison gown, believe me, my underwear will be something else. Next to my skin I'll be Queen of the Fairies. Oh, please don't be silly, Mummy, nobody will ever see it.

SCENE TWO

Evening

Melchior I'm bored. I've had enough of this game.

Otto If you stop, we all stop. What's our homework, Melchior, do you know?

Melchior Why don't you just carry on with the game.

Moritz Where are you going?

Melchior A walk maybe.

Georg But it's nearly dark. Have you done your homework already?

Melchior I like walking in the dark.

Ernst Central America. Louis the Fifteenth. Sixty lines of Homer. Seven equations.

Melchior To hell with homework.

Georg That Latin has to be in tomorrow.

Moritz Whatever you want to do, whatever you want to think – homework's there first, like a great crack in the earth at your feet.

Otto I'm off.

Georg Me too. Homework here I come.

Ernst And me.

Rilou Good night, Melchior.

Melchior Good night.

All go but Melchior and Moritz.

I wish to God I knew what we're doing on this earth!

Moritz Why do we have to go to school? I'd rather be a flea on a dog. Why do we go? To take exams. And why exams? So they can fail us. They have to fail seven of us. The class above only takes sixty. Seven of us have to evaporate. Ever since Christmas I've felt so peculiar, a bit desperate somehow – If it weren't for my father I'd be gone, bags packed and gone. I'd be in America.

Melchior Let's talk about something else.

Moritz Did you see that black cat?

Melchior You superstitious?

Moritz Ha, who knows? She came right over from the other side and crossed in front of us, tail up. Meaningless, of course.

Melchior You know what I think? All who scramble out of idiot religion topple headfirst into imbecile superstition. Let's sit under that big beech tree. This lovely warm wind is coming off the mountains. Do you know what I'd like to be? A tree spirit, a baby dryad. Up there in the highest branches, swayed and lulled and cradled the whole night.

Moritz Unbutton your jacket, Melchior.

Melchior Wonderful how this wind comes in under your clothes.

Moritz It's suddenly so dark. I can't see my hand in front of my face. Where've you gone? Melchior – don't you believe that man's sense of shame is completely artificial – manufactured by his upbringing?

Melchior The other day I was thinking about just that. I would say shame is rooted in human nature. You can't escape it. Imagine: you're ordered to take all your clothes off in front of your best friend. You wouldn't. Or you'd do it – only if he did exactly the same, at the same time.

Moritz If ever I have children they'll all sleep in the same room – right from the start. If possible, the same bed. Night and morning they'll help undress and dress each other – boys and girls, all together. In summer, when it's hot, they'll all wear a very simple short tunic – white linen or something of that sort – light and simple. Fastened with leather thongs. Think how those children would grow up – so relaxed and easy with each other. And look at us.

4

Melchior You're right, Moritz. I'm sure you are. The only snag is – what happens when the girls get pregnant?

Moritz What do you mean? Get pregnant?

Melchior Instinct, Moritz. That's one thing we have to believe in, like it or not. The instinctive drives. Suppose you shut up a tom-cat and a female cat together, from birth, for life, no other cats near them, never a glimpse of one other cat – nothing in there with them but their own drives. What happens? One day, bang, the female's pregnant. And neither of them ever got a hint how to do it from any other cat. Not one lesson.

Moritz Yes, well, that's animals. I'm sure it's that way with animals.

Melchior And not humans? Think how it's going to be, Moritz, when all your boys and girls are tangled happily together in that big bed of yours. One night one of the boys begins to dream and he wakes up fairly bursting with instinct. With the male drive, Moritz. I'll bet you –

Moritz All right. All right. Maybe you're right. Even so –

Melchior And when your girls get to the same point – do you suppose one or two ideas don't come bubbling up for them too? I know girls are slightly different – it's not quite the same – In fact, the truth is we don't quite know, do we? But we can assume. Can't we assume? The physical moment, the idea, the big bed – and curiosity does the rest.

Moritz One question.

Melchior Yes?

Moritz Promise you'll answer.

Melchior Of course.

Moritz Promise.

Melchior Yes, I promise. What is it?

Moritz Have you done that Latin homework?

Melchior Moritz, nobody can hear us. Spit it out. What is it?

Moritz These children of mine, they will have to spend the whole day working, quite hard – in the yard or the garden. Or playing energetic games, the most strenuous games. Horse-riding, gymnastics, rock-climbing. Then they'll really sleep. They'll go deep, deep down – utterly exhausted. When you're deeply asleep, truly asleep – I don't think you dream at all. We're so pampered and spoiled, half the night we're dreaming.

Melchior From now on till after the grape harvest I'm sleeping in my hammock. I've stowed my bed away. It folds up. I had the weirdest dream last winter: I was flogging our dog, Lolo, so hard and so long, in the end he couldn't move a limb. The most horrible dream I ever had. Why are you staring at me like that?

Moritz Have you felt it?

Melchior Felt what?

Moritz What was it you called it?

Melchior The male drive?

Moritz That.

Melchior Ha! And how.

Moritz Me too.

Melchior As a matter of fact, I've been experiencing it for quite some time . . . a year.

Moritz I thought I'd been hit by lightning.

Melchior Was it a dream?

Moritz Funny, just a flash – There were these legs in sky-blue tights climbing over the teacher's desk – To tell you the truth, I thought they were – I just got a glimpse.

Melchior Georg Zirschnitz dreams about his mother.

Moritz He told you that?

Melchior On the road out to the old Gallows Hill.

Moritz Ever since that night – if you knew what I've been through.

Melchior Bad conscience?

Moritz Absolute death-agony.

Melchior Oh, my God.

Moritz I thought I'd caught some ghastly disease. I thought I was going rotten inside, falling to bits inside. Then I started writing it all up in my diary – that seemed to calm me down a bit. Melchior – this last three weeks, talk about Agony in the Garden!

Melchior I was better prepared for it. I felt a bit ashamed, but that was all.

Moritz And you're nearly a year younger than me.

Melchior I wouldn't worry. According to all my experience, there is no particular age at which this phantom first appears. You know Lammermeier – he's three years older than me. Hanschen Rilow says he still dreams about chocolate éclairs and apricot jam.

Moritz How does Rilow know that?

Melchior He asked him.

Moritz Asked him! I wouldn't dare ask anybody.

Melchior You asked me.

Moritz So I did. Isn't this a very strange game they're playing with us, Melchior? All these things being done to us. And we're supposed to be glad. Supposed even to be grateful. I'd never felt anything like it before – such a craving – for such unbearable excitements. Unbearable! Why wasn't I left to sleep through it – and wake up when it was all over? My parents could have had countless children who would have pleased them better than I do. Maybe I'm the most evil one they could have had. But here I am. And God knows where I came from or how I got here. Yet I'm supposed to justify my being here. To myself, to everybody. How did we ever come to wake up in this morass? Did you never try to puzzle it out, Melchior?

Melchior Is this something else you don't know yet?

Moritz Where could I get to know? Oh, yes, chickens lay eggs, I've seen that. And Mama's supposed to have carried me around somewhere under her heart – so I've been told. But isn't there a bit more to it? You know how the Queen of Hearts shows her bare shoulders right down to –? When I was only four or five, I used to dread anybody turning that card up – She made me feel so – God knows, awful. I've got over that, but I can hardly speak to a girl without my brains going into a kind of spin down a drain – I think the most horrible things, and I swear, Melchior, I swear I've no idea what they are. It's all just horrible.

Melchior I will explain everything. From beginning to end. Some of it I got from books. Some of it from pictures. And some from observing the natural world. It will amaze you. It knocked religion out of me, I can tell you. I told Georg Zirschnitz. He wanted to tell Rilow, but do you know what? Rilow had it all from his governess, years ago.

Moritz I've been through the encyclopedia from A to Z. Huge, ponderous volumes, solid with words. Masses and masses and masses of words. But not one plain description of what actually goes on. It's this weird feeling of – shame. What's the point of an encyclopedia that gives you the answers to everything – except the most basic question of life.

Melchior You've seen two dogs in the street?

Moritz Stop. That's enough. Nothing more today, Melchior. I've still got Central America, and Louis the Fifteenth, and sixty lines of Homer, and seven equations – and the Latin prose. Otherwise, tomorrow I've had it. If I'm going to deal with all that tonight, I need to be dumb as an ox. So please, Melchior.

Melchior Come to my room. In three-quarters of an hour I'll see to your Homer, the equations and two Latin proses. I'll chuck in a few mistakes for you. And that will be it. Mama will make us some fresh lemonade and you and I, Moritz – we'll have a cosy little chat about sexual reproduction.

Moritz I can't. I can't just have a 'cosy little chat about sexual reproduction'. The only way I could take it would be – if you wrote it all out, Melchior, like instructions. That would really help me, I think. Write down all you know about it, very simple, but really clear. And put it among my books, tomorrow, during gym. Then I'll take it home not even knowing it's there. I'll come across it unexpectedly. My poor weary eyes won't be able to avoid giving it a glance. If you feel it's absolutely vital, you could put some diagrams in the margins.

Melchior Moritz, you're behaving like a girl. But if that's the way you want it . . . I'm sure it's going to be a very interesting exercise. One question, though, Moritz.

Moritz Hm?

Melchior Have you ever seen a girl's body?

Moritz Of course.

Melchior I mean with nothing on.

Moritz Stark naked.

Melchior So have I. Then I shan't need to provide illustrations.

Moritz It was in Leilich's anatomical museum during the shooting match. If I'd been caught, I'd have been thrown out of school. Right there in broad daylight – incredibly lifelike.

Melchior Last summer when I was in Frankfurt with Mama – Are you going?

Moritz I've got to get that homework done. Good night.

Melchior Goodbye, Moritz.

SCENE THREE

Wendla, Martha and Thea: stormy day.

Martha How the water gets into your shoes!

Wendla How the wind buffets your face!

Thea How your heart hammers and hammers!

Wendla Let's go to the bridge. Ilse said there's a flood – trees and bushes are being swept away. The boys have a raft out on it. They say Melchior Gabor nearly got drowned last night.

Thea He's a good swimmer.

Martha He's a wonderful swimmer!

Wendla Well, if he weren't he'd be dead.

Thea Your braid's coming loose, Martha – your braid's coming loose.

Martha Oh, let it, stupid thing. It's forever in the way. Such a nuisance! They won't let me wear my hair short, like yours. Or all free, like Wendla's. I can't have a fringe. Even at home I have to keep it all done up – because of my aunt.

Wendla I'll bring my scissors to Religious Instruction tomorrow. And while you're reciting 'Happy are they who walk in the paths of righteousness' – one big snip and your whole braid will be gone.

Martha For God's sake, Wendla, don't scare me. My father would hammer me black and blue. And my mother would lock me up three days in the coal shed.

Wendla What does he beat you with, Martha?

Martha I sometimes think they actually need a pest like me simply for shouting at and beating. If they didn't have me, they'd feel something missing in their lives.

Thea You poor thing.

Martha Are you allowed to thread a sky-blue ribbon through the top of your night-dress?

Thea Only pink satin. Mama says it goes with my jet-black eyes.

Martha I liked blue. It looked really pretty. But Mama whipped back the blankets and dragged me out of bed by my braid. I went smack down hands-and-knees on to the floor. Mama prays with us, you see – every night.

Wendla In your shoes, I'd have run off long ago.

Martha 'So that's what you're up to,' she screams. 'I see. I see where it's all leading. But you'll learn – Oh, yes, you'll learn. Then you'll know just how right your mother was – And so will she, poor woman, her conscience will be clear!'

Thea Heuargh!

Martha What do you suppose she means, Thea? What am I going to learn?

Thea She sounds mad. What do you think she meant, Wendla?

Wendla I would have asked her.

Martha I'm lying there, crying and wailing, and in comes Papa. One rip – and my night-gown's gone. I'm curled up on the floor, stripped and freezing. And he's roaring at me: 'There's the door! There's the street! Why don't you just walk straight out exactly as you are?'

Wendla I can't believe this.

Martha I was crouching, shivering – I had my head right down. Suddenly he grabbed me and shoved me into a sack. I spent the whole night in a sack.

Thea Slept the whole night in a sack? I could never do that.

Wendla Oh, if only I could take your place, Martha, and do it for you –

Martha It's the beatings I can't stand.

Thea But wouldn't you suffocate in a sack?

Martha Your head's left out. It's tied under your chin.

Thea Then they beat you?

Martha No. Only if there's a special reason.

Wendla What do they beat you with, Martha? What do they use?

Martha Anything. Does your mother think it's wrong to eat a piece of bread in bed?

Wendla Good Lord, no.

Martha They enjoy it. They don't talk about it, but I'm sure they love doing it. When I have children, I shall let them grow up like the weeds in our garden. Everybody ignores them and they grow tall and thick. But the roses – all staked out, trained on frames, fertilized, pruned, cut back and cut back, and worried about. Every year they look sicker. Then one spring they just don't seem to make it. And it's obvious they're dead.

Thea When I have children, I shall dress them head to foot in pink. Pink hats, pink dresses, pink shoes. Apart from their stockings – their stockings will be coal-black. And when I take them out, they'll all march in a line in front of me. How will you dress yours, Wendla?

Wendla What makes you so sure you're going to have children?

Thea Why shouldn't we?

Martha Aunt Euphemia hasn't got any.

Thea Don't be idiotic. How could she? She isn't married.

Wendla My Aunt Bauer's been married three times and she has no children.

Martha But if you did have children, Wendla, which would you rather have, boys or girls?

Wendla Boys! Boys!

Thea Me too. Boys every time.

Martha Me too! Twenty boys rather than three girls.

Thea Girls are boring.

Martha If I weren't already a girl, I would never want to be one.

Wendla I think, Martha, that is a question of taste. For me – every single day I thank God I am a girl. I honestly do. I wouldn't swap sexes, even with a prince. Even so, I still want to have boys.

Thea But that's really silly, Wendla. It's illogical.

Wendla My dear child, do you think so? It is a thousand times better to be loved by a man than by a woman. It's more ennobling.

Thea Are you saying that Pfille, the young trainee forester, loves Melitta in some more uplifting way than she loves him?

Wendla Yes, I am. Pfille has great pride. He's proud that he's the trainee forester. He's proud that he'll become a forester. Because Pfille has nothing else. But Melitta – all that Melitta can be proud about is what Pfille gives her. And he gives her a thousand times more than she had – so she's ecstatic.

Martha But, Wendla, aren't you proud of being yourself?

Wendla That really would be silly.

Martha If I were in your shoes, I'd be proud.

Thea Just see how she walks – look at her, Martha. What poise! And you have a very bold, straight look, Wendla. I'd say that's being proud.

Wendla Why should I be proud? I'm simply glad I'm a girl. If I weren't a girl, I'd kill myself, so that next time –

14

Melchior passes and waves.

Thea Oh, he's such a handsome boy.

Martha When they talk about Alexander the Great as a marvellous youth – that's how I imagine him.

Thea Ugh, Greek history! All I remember is how Socrates lay in a barrel while Alexander sold him the donkey's shadow.

Wendla They say he's the third best in his class.

Thea Professor Knockenbruch thinks he could be top if he wanted.

Martha He has a very attractive face. But I always think his friend looks more sensitive, more soulful.

Thea Moritz Steifel? That boy is an utter cretin.

Martha I've always liked him.

Thea He always manages to make me squirm somehow, wherever I meet him. At that children's party the Rilows gave, he offered me some chocolate. Can you imagine, Wendla, it was all soft and sticky. Isn't that just – He said he'd had it too long in his trouser pocket.

Wendla Do you know what Melchi Gabor said to me at that party? He told me he doesn't believe in anything. Not in God. Not in the beyond. Not in anything on earth.

SCENE FOUR

Boys in front of school.

Melchior Does anybody know where Moritz Steifel is?

Georg He's in for it now – Oh, boy, is he in for it!

Otto One of these days Steifel will go too far and that will be . . .

Georg I'm glad I'm not in his shoes, I can tell you.

Otto What a nerve! It's unbelievable.

Melchior What is? What's going on? What's happened?

Georg Don't ask *me* for bad news.

Otto I'm saying nothing.

Melchior Look, if somebody can't tell me straight out –

Robert All right. Moritz Steifel broke into the staff room.

Melchior He did what?

Otto He broke into the staff room. After the Latin lesson.

Georg He was last out. He stayed behind on purpose.

Otto I saw him. I was just coming round the corner along the corridor as he opened the door.

Melchior Jesus Christ!

Otto Ha! He'll need Jesus all right. One of the staff must have left the key in the door.

Rilow It wouldn't surprise me if Steifel has a skeleton key.

Otto That would be just like Steifel.

Georg Bit of luck it won't be much – Sunday afternoon detention. And a black mark on his report.

Otto Unless he gets kicked out of school altogether. He just might.

Rilow Here he is now.

Melchior White as a ghost!

Georg Moritz, what have you done?

Moritz Nothing. Absolutely nothing.

Otto You're trembling.

Moritz With happiness – with joy. I'm trembling with joy.

Otto They caught you?

Moritz I've passed, Melchior. I've passed. Now the whole world can go to hell. I have passed. Who'd have thought I'd ever pass. I still can't believe it. I had to go through the list again and again – and I'm there. My name's there. In black and white. Written with a finger of fire. Holy God, I can't believe it, I've passed. I feel peculiar. My head's reeling a bit. Melchior, oh, Melchior – if only you knew what it's been like!

Rilow Congratulations, Moritz. Just be thankful you got away with it.

Moritz Hanschen, you don't understand what was at stake. You cannot possibly know. This last three weeks I've been creeping past that door as if it were the jaws of hell. And today I happened to notice – it was open, just a crack. Unlocked. Nobody could have stopped me, not if they'd offered me a million. Nothing could have stopped me. Before I know it, there I am in the middle of the room, staring at the register. I open it. Turn the pages. Find the page – and the whole time – God, I'm still trembling –

Melchior Go on – the whole time?

Moritz The whole time the door behind me is gaping wide open. I can't remember how I got out and down those stairs.

Rilow Did Ernst Robel pass too?

Moritz Yes, yes, Robel's passed too. I saw his name.

Rilow Your head was spinning a bit too much, Steifel.

Robel's name can't have been there. If you knock out the complete dunces, with you and Robel there's sixty-one of us. The class upstairs takes only sixty. Sixty's the limit.

Moritz No, he was there. I saw his name as clear as my own. We're both going up. But for us two, it's provisional. They'll decide which of us to keep during the first term. Poor old Robel. I don't have to worry – I've seen the bottom of the pit, I know what's needed.

Otto I bet you five pounds, Steifel, that it will be you who will have to give way to Robel.

Moritz You can't afford it – and I'd prefer not to rob a beggar. My God, see me slog from now on. Let me tell you something – I don't mind telling you all now it doesn't matter – but I'd made my mind up. If I hadn't passed, I was going to shoot myself.

Otto Big-headed bullshitter!

Georg You daren't even pick up a gun. What you really need is a good smack in the face.

Melchior (*giving him one*) Come on, Moritz. Let's go to the forester's lodge.

Georg You don't swallow all that garbage of his, do you?

Melchior What's it got to do with you? Come on, Moritz. Let them say what they like. Let's get out of here.

Professors go by.

Professor Knockenbruch My dear fellow, look there. My best pupil and my worst. And yet those two are the closest pair of friends in my class. Incomprehensible!

Professor Hungergurt My dear fellow, I do agree, it is incomprehensible. Quite incomprehensible.

Melchior and Wendla meet in the wood.

Melchior Is that you, Wendla? What are you doing up here? Are you alone? I've been roaming about in this wood the last three hours without meeting one soul and suddenly – you burst out of the thicket like something in a folk-tale.

Wendla Well, it's only me.

Melchior Wendla Bergman. If I didn't know you so well, I would have to say you must be a dryad, fallen out of the high branches.

Wendla No, no – it's the same old Wendla Bergman. What are you doing here anyway?

Melchior I'm on the trail of my thoughts.

Wendla Well, I'm on the trail of woodruff. Mama wants it for her May brew. She meant to come with me but then at the last minute Aunt Bauer turned up and she can't face the hill – so here I am alone.

Melchior Have you found any?

Wendla A basketful – look. Over there by that beech it's thick as clover. And now I'm trying to find my way out of this wood. But I seem to be lost. What's the time?

Melchior Just gone half-past three. When do they expect you?

Wendla Only half-past three! I lay on the moss by the stream for I don't know how long – I had such a daydream, I just floated off. It seemed like ages. When I came to, I felt sure it must be evening.

Melchior You've plenty of time. Let's sit here for a bit.

This is my favourite spot, this bank, under the oak here. I love this place. If you lean your head back against the trunk and look up into the sky through the leaves, you can go into a trance. Feel the ground, it's still warm from the sun. Wendla, do you mind if I ask you something. I've been wanting to ask you for weeks.

Wendla I have to be home by five.

Melchior I'll show you the way, don't worry. And I'll carry your basket. We'll beat a path through the undergrowth along the old river-bed – we'll be at the bridge in ten minutes. When you're lying here, with your head propped, you get the most peculiar ideas, believe me.

Wendla So what was the question?

Melchior I've heard you go visiting very poor people. Taking them food, clothes, even money. Is that your idea or does your mother send you?

Wendla Oh, Mother sends me usually. They're families of labourers, with hordes of children. Their fathers can't find any work. So there's no food. No heating. No new clothes ever. And our house is so crammed with stuff, spilling out of wardrobes and cupboards. But why do you want to know?

Melchior When your mother sends you on errands of that kind – are you quite happy to go? Or do you feel reluctant?

Wendla Of course I'm happy to go. How could I not be?

Melchior But the children are dirty. The women are sick. The houses are full of filth, you can see that just in passing. The men hate you because you're well off and don't work.

Wendla But that's not true. And if it were true, it wouldn't make any difference. I'd be even more determined.

Melchior What do you mean, 'even more determined'?

Wendla I'd be even more determined to go. I'd get all the more pleasure out of being able to help them. Nothing would stop me.

Melchior So. You visit the poor because you get pleasure out of it.

Wendla I visit them because they're poor, Melchior.

Melchior But you wouldn't go if it gave you no pleasure.

Wendla Can I help it if it gives me pleasure?

Melchior So it gives you pleasure and at the same time gets you into heaven. Then I was right all the time. I've been chewing at this for the last month. A man doesn't have to be a miser to get no pleasure from visiting children who are sick and dirty.

Wendla I'm certain it would give you a great deal of pleasure.

Melchior And yet just because he gets no pleasure from it, that man is damned to hell for all eternity. I'm going to write an essay about this and give it to Pastor Kahbauch. He started me thinking about it. The way he blathers on about the joys of self-sacrifice. If he can't explain it all, then I'm finished with Sunday School and I shall never take confirmation.

Wendla But how could you do that to your parents? They would be mortified. Why not let yourself be confirmed. It's not the end of the world. If it weren't for the ridiculous clothes they make us wear, I could get quite excited about it.

Melchior Genuine self-sacrifice doesn't exist. There is no such thing as selflessness. I watch the good people, so admired by everybody and so pleased with their own self-righteousness. I see the bad people, condemned by everybody, grumbling and sulking about. And I see you, Wendla Bergman, shaking your curly hair and laughing – and all the time I feel so solemn and far-off, like an outcast. As if I were looking at you all from some other world. Tell me, Wendla, when you were lying by the stream there – what were you dreaming about?

Wendla Oh – just – nonsense really.

Melchior With your eyes wide open?!

Wendla I was dreaming I was a child beggar, dreadfully poor. Pushed out on to the street at five in the morning. And forced to beg all day – rain, snow, freezing wind, whatever. Begging from cold, heartless, hard-faced people. Then at night when I came back home, maybe soaked to the bone, frozen, faint with hunger – if I hadn't collected enough money to satisfy my father, then he'd beat me, he'd beat me and beat me and beat me –

Melchior Wendla, this is what those insipid, inane children's stories have filled you up with. Don't you know brutal fathers like that don't exist any more?

Wendla Oh, really? Well, you're wrong. They do exist. Martha Bessel gets beaten night after night. You can see the welts on her legs, all blue and red. The things that girl has to go through. It would make anybody sweat to hear her talk about it. I wake up at night thinking about her and I just cry. She's so pitiful. If only we could help her somehow. I would take her place for a week if I could – if that were possible, I'd gladly do it.

Melchior Her father should be reported. Then Martha would be taken away from him.

Wendla I have never been beaten, Melchior. Never once in my whole life. I can't even imagine what it would feel like.

I've tried beating myself, just to get some idea – it must be the most horrible feeling.

Melchior I cannot believe any child is ever the better for it.

Wendla Ever the better for what?

Melchior For being beaten.

Wendla I suppose this switch would be the sort of thing – tough and lithe.

Melchior That would draw blood.

Wendla Melchior, beat me with it – go on – just once.

Melchior Beat you?

Wendla Yes. Me. Now.

Melchior Wendla, what's got into you?

Wendla Why not?

Melchior Stop it, Wendla. I'm not going to beat you.

Wendla But I'm giving you permission.

Melchior No.

Wendla But what if I ask you to? Melchior!

Melchior Are you crazy?

Wendla Nobody's ever beaten me, ever, not once in my whole life.

Melchior If you can ask for something like that –

Wendla Please, Melchior, please.

Melchior Please? I'll teach you to say please.

Hits her with switch.

Wendla Oh, God! I can't feel it, I can't feel a thing!

Melchior That's because of all your skirts and your – all those underthings and protection –

Wendla My legs! Hit my legs!

Melchior Wendla!

Hits her harder.

Wendla You're only stroking me! That's not beating – that's stroking and tickling!

Melchior You witch! Just you wait! I'll thrash the devil out of you –

Attacks her with fists, etc. She screams. He attacks more violently – sudden sobbing fury. Breaks away and dashes off among trees – wild sobbing.

Act Two

SCENE ONE

Melchior's study. Melchior and Moritz.

Moritz I'm OK now. Bit jangled still maybe. During Greek I slept like the drunken one-eyed Polyphemus himself. I'm surprised old Zungenschlag didn't twist my ear. I only just managed to make it this morning. I was still thinking about the verbs ending in *mi* when I woke up. Then all through breakfast and all the way to school, conjugating those damned verbs. God almighty in heaven! Christ in hell, I felt my brains were going to seize up – my throat ached. I must have dropped off some time after three. My pen had made a great blot on the book. When Mathilde woke me, the blackbirds were singing in the garden under my window. It was just dawn. The lilac bushes are in full flower. And suddenly I felt terribly depressed. Just horribly – depressed. I can't really describe it. A very black feeling. But I did up my collar, smartened my hair – got control of myself. Going against your nature certainly wakens you up.

Melchior Shall I roll you a cigarette?

Moritz Thank you. But I don't think this is the moment to start smoking. I just want things to wobble along very steadily as they are. Just let me go on studying till my eyes burst. Already this term Robel's had six Fs. Three for Greek. Twice with old Knockenbruch. And the latest in Literature. I've only had five. And that's my last. From now on, not one more F for me. Robel will never blow his brains out. His parents aren't sacrificing everything for him. Whenever he feels like it, he can clear off and become a mercenary in some war. Or a cowboy. Or a seaman. But if I fail, my father drops down with a stroke and my mother's carried off screaming to the madhouse. So. We can't let that happen, can we? Before the exams I prayed. I asked God to give me tuberculosis – so this cup might pass from me untasted. Well, it did pass. For a while. It's still hovering there, though. I see its halo gleaming in the distance. I dare hardly lift my eyes. But now at least I've managed to grab the bottom rung of the ladder. Somehow I'll haul the rest of me up. I have to. One slip and I'm down there with a broken neck – absolutely without fail broken-necked and finished.

Melchior Life always has some nasty little joker hidden up its sleeve. I could think quite seriously of hanging myself from the branches. Wasn't my mother bringing us some tea?

Moritz Tea would be very welcome. Look at me, I'm trembling. I feel light-headed, sort of bodiless – the weirdest sensation. Just touch me. Everything's become very clear and sharp – I see and hear and feel everything incredibly clearly. Yet it's all very dreamy. The way the garden deepens away there under the moonlight – as if it went off into bottomless space. Such a deep, moody atmosphere. The silence is intense. Shadowy figures drift out from the bushes. They hurry away, writhing in a mysterious frenzy, quite soundless. A council of some kind is being held under that chestnut tree. Something is being decided. Let's go down and have a look, Melchior.

Melchior When we've had our tea maybe.

Moritz The leaves are moving ever so slightly. They'll be whispering something. Like my grandmother telling the story of the queen who had no head. Once upon a time, there was an incredibly beautiful queen, more dazzling than the sun. Not one girl in the whole kingdom could compare with her. Unfortunately, she had no head. She was born that way. So she couldn't eat, she couldn't drink, couldn't see, couldn't laugh. Couldn't kiss. The only way she could make herself understood to her court was through the gestures of her tiny soft hand. With her dainty little feet she tapped out declarations of war and sentences of death. One day her realm was conquered by a king who happened to have two heads. These two heads were at loggerheads day and night, year in year out, shouting each other down, yelling into each other's ears, deafening each other, deaf to each other. But now the court magician took the smaller of these two heads and gave it to the queen. And behold, it was a perfect fit. And suited her into the bargain. Then the king married the queen, and from that day the heads had not one cross word to say to each other. In fact, they kissed each other constantly on the brow, the eyelids, the tip of the nose and the mouth, and loved each other. Yes, and lived happily ever after. Christ, what a load of gibberish! But what does it mean, Melchior? All term this queen's been going through my head. I can't stop thinking about her. And if I see any girl that's half attractive – I imagine her without a head. Then suddenly I'm the headless queen. Me. There is a possibility, I suppose, that somebody will stick another head on my shoulders.

Frau Gabor brings tea.

Frau Gabor Here you are, children. Milk and sugar if you want it. Good evening, Herr Steifel. How are you?

Moritz Very well, thank you, Frau Gabor. I was watching the very strange things going on down there in the garden.

Frau Gabor You look rather pale. Are you feeling all right?

Moritz I've been having some late nights.

Melchior He worked all last night.

Frau Gabor Do you think that is wise, Herr Steifel? It is always good to remember priorities, and the first priority, I would say, is to protect your health. Young boys should take particular care. Schoolwork must never be allowed to come before health. Long walks in the fresh air – that's what's needed. Striding out and filling the lungs. Far more important at your age than burying yourself in medieval German.

Moritz You're quite right, Frau Gabor. Yes, strenuous walks! And one can do all kinds of work while walking. Why on earth haven't I thought of it before? There's always the written work, of course. That has to be done at home.

Melchior Do your written work here, with me. It would help both of us. Mama, did you hear that Max von Trenk died today? He had inflammation of the brain. At midday Hanschen Rilow came straight from von Trenk's deathbed to the headmaster to tell him that he'd just watched von Trenk die. 'Rilow!' barks Sonnenstich. 'You still owe two hours of detention from last week. Here's a note for your form master: See to it. Now, the whole class will attend the funeral.' Rilow couldn't believe it – he just stood there dumbstruck.

Frau Gabor What's the book, Melchior?

Melchior *Faust.*

Frau Gabor Have you read all of it?

Melchior Still some to go.

Moritz We've just got to the Walpurgisnacht scene.

Frau Gabor I think I might have waited a little longer before tackling a book like that. Two more years, perhaps.

Melchior Never in any book have I read passages of such intense beauty. Why shouldn't I read it?

Frau Gabor But so much of it, surely, is quite beyond the understanding of a young boy.

Melchior Mother, how can you know that? Of course, I realize only too well that I am not yet ready to grasp this work in all its sublimity.

Moritz We always read it together. That helps to open things up. Amazing how much.

Frau Gabor Melchior, I know you are old enough to distinguish between what is good for you and what is bad. And I know you are aware – we only do what we can take responsibility for. It means, of course, that one avoids anything of which one might be ashamed. I would be eternally grateful if you would never put me in the position of having to keep things from you. That goes without saying, of course. I merely want to remind you two boys that even the best book can be dangerous if we read it when we are too young. There are so many things that require maturity, and experience, if they are to be set in a proper perspective. I would always prefer to trust your good sense, Melchior, before any pedagogue's rigid set of rules. If either of you wants anything more, I shall be in my bedroom. (*She goes.*)

Moritz I think your mother's referring to the Gretchen story.

Melchior Well, we didn't get too hot and bothered about that, did we?

Moritz Not even Faust himself could have made less of it.

Melchior Whatever this great masterpiece amounts to, that disgraceful little episode is hardly the climax of it. If Faust promised to marry the girl, or if he just walked out and left her, either way he's equally guilty. But what if she did die of a broken heart, so what? Should I care? Yet everybody gets into such a state about it. They're so embarrassed. In the whole book, it's all they ever see – You'd think the thoughts of the entire world were fixated on a penis and a vagina.

Moritz Yes, well. Since I read that little essay of yours I think mine might be too. It dropped out at my feet, beginning of the holidays. I was opening my French grammar. I locked the door. And I stared at your lines. All the words seemed to be jumping up and down. I skimmed over them like a frightened owl flying through a burning forest. I think I read most of it with my eyes shut. Your explanations sounded so strange. At the same time – so familiar. Like memories somehow, things I could nearly remember but not quite. Like a song you hummed as a very small child – that you never heard again until you were on your deathbed, then you heard some very small child singing it. What disturbed me most was what you said about girls. That hit me very hard. Surely, Melchior, it's sweeter to suffer injustice than to be the one who acts unjustly. That's my idea of bliss – the peak of human bliss – to be innocent and yet to submit to – such a sweet wrong.

Melchior I don't want my bliss as a charity.

Moritz Why not?

Melchior I don't want anything I haven't had to fight for and win.

Moritz But is that pleasure, Melchior? The girl's pleasure – girls are like gods in their pleasures. A girl tries to protect herself, doesn't she? It's her instinct to resist. But right up to the very last moment, she suspends any resentment or fear or anger – so all at once she can see the heavens open and engulf her. And that's the moment when she most dreads hell and damnation – as her paradise bursts into flower. All her feelings unspoiled, fresh, astonishing to her – like a spring gushing out of a rock. She lifts a cup – no human lip has ever touched it – a great goblet of nectar, flaming and flickering, and she drains it, gulp after gulp. Well, compared to that, how flat and pitiful must a man's pleasure be.

Melchior Think whatever you like, but keep it to yourself. I don't even let myself think about it.

SCENE TWO

Bergmans' living-room.

Frau Bergman Wendla! Wendla!

Wendla Mother?

Frau Bergman Oh, you're up. What a good child you are!

Wendla Have you been out already?

Frau Bergman Quickly, go and get dressed. I want you to hurry over to Ina's with this basket.

Wendla Have you seen her? How is she? Is she any better?

Frau Bergman Oh, Wendla, just think. Last night she was visited by the stork. It brought her a baby boy.

Wendla A baby boy? Oh, wonderful! Oh, a baby boy! That explains it. That's why she's had that awful flu for so long –

Frau Bergman A most beautiful baby boy!

Wendla I have to see it. Mother, that makes me an aunt for the third time. An aunt to one girl and two boys.

Frau Bergman And what boys they are, Wendla! That's what comes of living right next to the church. Tomorrow will be two years to the day when she walked up the aisle in her white lace.

Wendla Were you there when the stork brought him?

Frau Bergman It had just flown away. How about pinning a rose on your dress?

Wendla Oh, why didn't you get there earlier, Mother?

Frau Bergman As a matter of fact, I believe he brought something for you too – a brooch, I think.

Wendla Oh, Mother, what a pity!

Frau Bergman What's the matter? I'm sure it will be quite a nice brooch.

Wendla I don't want any more brooches.

Frau Bergman Then what do you want?

Wendla I want to know whether the stork flew down the chimney or in through the window.

Frau Bergman You'd better ask Ina. Ask Ina, my treasure, and she'll tell you. She talked to him for a good half-hour.

Wendla Yes, as soon as I get over there I'll ask Ina.

Frau Bergman Don't forget, my sweet, will you? Then you can tell me, because I'd like to know too – which way does the stork come in? Down the chimney or in through the window?

Wendla Wouldn't it be better to ask the chimney sweep? He'd be the one to know, wouldn't he? If it comes down the chimney?

Frau Bergman Heavens, child, don't you go asking the chimney sweep anything of the kind. What on earth could the chimney sweep know about the stork? He'll just give you nonsense – a whole string of absurdities . . . that he doesn't even believe himself. What are you looking at, Wendla?

Wendla Mother, there's a man – he's three times the size of an ox. His feet are as huge as river barges.

Frau Bergman What are you saying? There must be –

Wendla He's holding a bedstead under his chin like a fiddle, and he's playing 'The Watch on the Rhine' – Oh, you're too late, he's gone round the corner.

Frau Bergman Oh, you little devil! Giving your poor, simple mother a shock like that! Go on, away with you. Don't forget your hat. When will you grow up, Wendla? I've almost given up hope that you ever will.

Wendla So have I, Mother. On the growing-up front, my prospects seem quite bleak. Here's my sister married two years, she's already made me an aunt three times over – and I still haven't the faintest idea how it happens. Oh, don't get cross, Mummy, please don't get cross. Who else can I ask if I can't ask you? Tell me, Mummy, tell me. How does it all happen? I'm fourteen. I'm too old to believe in storks coming down chimneys.

Frau Bergman Dear God, what a strange wilful daughter I have. The things you come out with. I could not possibly do that, Wendla.

Wendla But why not, Mother? Why not? If everyone is so wildly happy with the results, why can't it be spelt out plain and simple? It can't be so dreadful.

Frau Bergman Oh, God in heaven, what have I done to deserve this? Please, please, dear child, go and get your coat on.

Wendla I'm going. But what if your dear child goes straight to the chimney sweep?

Frau Bergman Do you want to drive me mad, Wendla? Oh, my sweet darling, come here, come. I'll tell you everything – dear God, but not today Wendla. Tomorrow or perhaps the day after. Or some time next week, one day next week. Whenever you like. Oh, my little girl! My darling!

Wendla Today. Now. Right now. Mother, after I've seen how it upsets you, what am I to think? I'll never be able to rest now till I know everything.

Frau Bergman I can't, Wendla.

Wendla Mother, look. You sit here. And I'll kneel down here. And I'll put my head in your lap, like this. And you pull your apron over my head – then you can simply talk. As if the room were empty. Just say everything. I shan't flinch. I shan't yell out or run screaming. Whatever happens, I'll stay right here where I am.

Frau Bergman God knows, I'm not to blame, Wendla. Heaven is my witness, none of it is my fault. Oh, for God's sake – yes, yes, all right, I'll tell you where you came from. Now. Well, Wendla, you see –

Wendla (*under apron*) I'm listening.

Frau Bergman I can't. Oh, my little treasure, I simply can't. I can't take the responsibility for it. I ought to be thrown into a prison. You ought to be taken away from me –

Wendla Be brave, Mother.

Frau Bergman Very well. So. Are you listening?

Wendla Oh, God.

Frau Bergman If you want to have a baby – can you hear me, Wendla?

Wendla Mother, I can't bear this very much longer. Will you hurry up and say it.

Frau Bergman To have a baby, you have to love the man – the man to whom you are married – you have to love him, truly love him in the way that only a woman loves a man. You have to love him so much – with all your heart and all your – so much – it's – it's simply unutterable. You have to love him in a way that's not possible for a girl of your age. And – that's it. There.

Wendla (*getting up*) Great God in heaven!

Frau Bergman So now you know what trials lie in wait for you.

Wendla And there's nothing more to it?

Frau Bergman As God is my witness! Now take the basket and off to Ina's. She'll give you chocolate. And there'll be cake. Let's look at you. Laced boots, silk gloves, sailor dress, a rose in your hair. That little skirt's so pretty but, oh, Wendla, it is getting far too short. It truly is.

Wendla Have you already bought the meat for lunch, Mother?

Frau Bergman Well, God bless you. I really shall have to tack a few inches on to that hem.

SCENE THREE

Rilow in lavatory. He lifts toilet seat.

Rilow Have you prayed tonight, Desdemona?

Takes from under his shirt the Venus of Palma Vecchi.

You don't seem to be praying very hard, my lovely – so deliciously contemplating all that is still to come – Just as in that moment of our first encounter, that wave of rapture when I spied you in the window of Schlesinger's shop – between a brass candlestick and a hunting knife. Those flowering limbs, just as they were then, the swelling, soft curve of your hips, those girlish breasts, so eager, so unworldly, not one bit less alluring. How giddy with joy that painter must have been when his fourteen-year-old model lay there lolling across the divan, right in front of his eyes – he could reach out and touch her.

Will you visit me in my dreams sometimes? I shall rise in the warm bed, my arms outstretched, and I'll kiss you till you gasp. You shall take possession of me – as the heiress takes possession of her derelict castle, when doors and gates swing open to invisible hands, and down in the park, once more, the fountain begins to jet and splash –

It is the cause, it is the cause –

This dreadful pounding in my chest should assure you, I do not murder you lightly. My larynx goes tight when I think of all my lonely nights. I swear on my soul, dear child, it is no exhaustion of my desire, no surfeit of your body, that drives me to this act. What man could ever be sated with you?

No. Your monstrous chastity demands too much. You dry up the marrow in my bones, you soften my spine, you fog the sparkle in my young eyes. These unmoving limbs of yours have worn me out. One of us must die. And the victory – has to be mine.

How many like you have gone this way before you? How many beauties have I grappled with on this brink, in this same struggle? First came Thumann's 'Psyche' – a legacy from the shrivelled-up Mademoiselle Angélique, that old rattlesnake in the paradise of my childhood. Correggio's 'Io'. Lossow's 'Galatea'. Then that 'Amor' by Bouguereau. 'Ada' by J. van Beers – the very 'Ada' I had to abduct from the secret drawer of my father's desk, to add to my harem. And that shuddering, ecstatic 'Leda' by Makart. She fell out from my brother's college notes when I was inspecting his progress. That's six. Six before you who paused here, as you do now, staring into the bowels of hell – about to plunge. Let the fact console you. Don't use that imploring gaze to lash my agonies out of control.

You are not dying for your sins. You are dying for mine. Simply to save myself, with my heart ripped wide open, I commit this *crime passionnel* – for the seventh time. Necessity! Bluebeard's role is tragic. I cannot believe that the suffering of all his murdered wives added up to anything like his when he strangled only one.

But my conscience will recover. And so will my body. Yes, my vigour will return when you, my voluptuous little she-devil, no longer repose in my red-silk-lined jewel case. I think I'll replace you with the 'Lorelei' of Bodenhausen. Or perhaps with Linger's 'Forsaken Woman'. Then again, I might nestle 'Loni' of Defregger into that sumptuous, secret apartment. Those ladies will soon refresh me. Another three months of your unveiled holy of holies, my darling soul, would have melted my brains like a butter pat on a grilled fish. The time has come to separate the bed from the banquet.

Those insatiable Roman emperors are alive in me. She who is about to die – salutes me. Woman, woman, why do your knees embrace each other so tightly? Kiss each other so closely? Even now, as you stare into the unfathomable – the everlasting. One kindly lift of an eyelid and I'll reprieve you. One amorous sigh stirring your cool pose, one gleam of lust in your painted eye – The slightest softening of your mouth towards me, O woman, and I will frame you in gold, I'll hang you above my bed. Can't you see? Can't you guess? What's driving me mad is nothing but your chastity.

Yes, and for that I curse you. I curse all monsters of your type. Her impeccable breeding is all too apparent. It never wavers for a moment. No more than does mine –

Have you prayed tonight, Desdemona?

My heart's clenched in a cramp – Ah! What of it! St Agnes also died for chastity – in a brothel – and she wasn't half as nude as you are, wrapped in her saintly hair. With a single stroke they swept off her head. One more kiss. Your body is all blossoms. These dainty breasts. These moulded, smooth, torturing knees –

It is the cause, it is the cause, my soul;
Let me not name it to you, you chaste stars!
It is the cause.

He drops the picture into the depths. Closes the toilet lid.

SCENE FOUR

Melchior in hayloft. Wendla comes up ladder.

Wendla So here you are. Everybody's looking for you. The wagon's gone out again. Come on, you're needed. Some nasty-looking clouds are piling up – there's a storm coming.

Melchior Get away from me. Keep away.

Wendla What's the matter with you? Why are you huddling over there?

Melchior Get away – or I'll throw you down on to the threshing floor.

38

Wendla You're not going to order me. If I want to stay, I stay. Come out into the meadows with me, Melchior. It's all gloomy and dank in here. And what if we do get soaked in the rain – that will be lovely too.

Melchior Smell this hay! Isn't it the most thrilling smell? The sky outside there must be black as the pit. All I can see is your rose. It seems to glow. And your heart – I can hear your heart beating. All I can hear is your heart beating.

Wendla Don't kiss me, Melchior. Don't kiss me!

Melchior Your heart – I can hear your heart!

Wendla Oh, don't kiss – people love each other if they kiss. No, Melchior, no!

Melchior There's no such thing as love. It doesn't exist. Self-interest is everything. I don't love you any more than you love me.

Wendla Please, Melchior, please!

Melchior Wendla!

Wendla Don't, Melchior, don't. No, no, no, no.

SCENE FIVE

Frau Gabor (*reading over the letter she has just composed*) Dear Herr Steifel,
   During this last twenty-four hours I have gone over everything in your letter again and again, and I have thought about it deeply and seriously. It is with a heavy heart that I take up my pen to reply. On my word of honour, I am simply unable to furnish you with the money necessary for your fare to Amsterdam. Not only do I have no such sum of ready cash to hand, but even if I had it, I would regard myself as not so much irresponsible as

39

positively wicked, and I would even say in the highest degree sinful, if I were to provide you with the means of taking such a reckless and almost certainly catastrophic step. You would be doing me great wrong, Herr Steifel, if you were to interpret this response to your appeal as an indication of coldness in my feelings towards you. Quite the opposite. But I would be guilty of the grossest dereliction of my duties as a parent and an adult if I were to allow your temporary confusion to make me lose my head and leave me at the mercy of natural instinct. Perhaps you would like me to write to your mother and father. I would do so gladly if you think it could be of any help. In any case, I shall do all I can to convince them of how you have driven yourself without respite during this last term. And I shall certainly let them know that to judge you too severely for what has happened would be, in my opinion, most unfair to you, and, much more important, given your distressed and exhausted condition, could easily do untold damage to your physical and mental well-being.

But there is one thing further I feel I must mention. I was most startled, Herr Steifel, by your barely concealed threat to do away with yourself if the means for your escape should be on this occasion denied. No matter how disproportionate problems may seem, one ought never to permit oneself even to consider such an ignoble solution to them. I am especially unhappy about one particular aspect of the matter. Herr Steifel, I have never shown you anything but kindness and yet I can only read this threat as an apparent attempt to make me responsible for the unthinkably blasphemous action that you seem now to be contemplating. Less sympathetic witnesses could even take a graver view. They might well regard it as nothing less than deliberate blackmail. I must confess that you – who have always exemplified the highest ideals of honourable and correct behaviour – were the very last person from whom I would have expected this.

For that reason I am confident that my letter will find you in a more reasonable frame of mind, with something of your normal outlook restored. You must face the situation and deal with it. To evaluate a young man by his school report is, in my opinion, most misleading. We have no lack of precedents for bad scholars who become distinguished pillars of society and, conversely, brilliant scholars who in later life achieve nothing of note. But let me conclude with a warm assurance: as far as lies in my power, your relationship with Melchior need be in no way affected by your present difficulties. I shall continue to derive the greatest pleasure from seeing my son accompanied by a young man for whom, no matter how the world may choose to condemn him, I have always felt the fondest regard.

So chin up, Herr Steifel. Disasters of one sort or another take us all by surprise and have to be overcome. If everyone went straight to the poison bottle or the dagger, this world of ours would soon be empty. Let me hear from you again soon. With warmest greetings from your ever-devoted maternal friend – Fanny G.

SCENE SIX

The Bergmans' garden in the morning.

Wendla Why did you creep away out of the drawing-room? To look for violets? Because Mother will see me smiling. Why can't you control your lips any more? I don't know. What is happening to me? I don't know and I just can't find words for the feeling –

The path is like velvet. Not a pebble. Not a thorn. My feet barely touch the earth. Oh, what a magical deep sleep I had last night.

This is where they were. I feel so strange – solemn. Like a nun at Communion. Lovely violets. No, Mummy, be calm. I'll wear the long prison-gown now. Oh, God, if only somebody would come and let me fling my arms around their neck and tell them everything –

Overcast sky at dusk. Path winding through marshy undergrowth. Sound of a river.

Moritz It has to be this way. I don't fit in. And if they all go crazy, I just can't care any more. I'm going to shut the door behind me. I'm going to step out – for freedom. I'm finished with being pushed around.

I've never imposed myself on anybody. So why should I start now? I have no contract with our dear Lord. However you look at this whole business, it all boils down to one thing. The pressure. I don't blame my parents. Even so, they must have had some inkling, they must have been ready for the worst. They're old enough to know what they were doing. When I came into the world, I was only an ignorant babe – otherwise I'd have had the wit to become somebody else. Yet why should I have to pay the penalty for the fact that all the places were already filled up?

When I was born, I must have dropped out on my head. Somebody gives you a mad dog, unasked for, as a present. You give a mad dog back. But when he refuses to take his mad dog back, I'm the one who – does nothing, doesn't insist, puts up with it. I must have been dropped on my head.

Being born is laughable – it's nothing but pure chance. Yet no matter how you weigh it all up and reckon all the factors, still we're supposed to hold it sacred, and we commit a horrible sin if we – it's enough to make you laugh your head right off!

At least the weather's being cooperative. Rain threatened all day, but it was still nice and fine towards evening. Nature was very strangely peaceful. Nothing jarred. Nothing was out of place. Everything fitted perfectly together. Sky and earth were like one giant spider's web – with the light coming through. And everything seemed to be so much at ease. The whole landscape so soft – like a lullaby: 'Sleep, little princeling, sleep on'. Fräulein Snandulia sang that. Pity about her ridiculous elbows. We danced at that party on St Cecilia's day. Fräulein Snandulia dances only in groups. Her silk gown was cut very low at the back – and at the front. Right down to her waist at the back. And at the front – so far down it made your head swim. I don't think she had anything on at all underneath it.

Well, that would be one good reason not to. I'm curious mainly. It must be such a peculiar sensation – like going over a waterfall. I shan't be coming back to tell them I still haven't done it. There's something quite unbearable about it – to be a human being – who has never done the most human thing of all. 'So, my dear chap, back from Egypt and never saw the pyramids? Well, well, well –'

Anyway, no more crying today, Moritz. And no more thinking about my funeral. Melchior will put a wreath on my coffin. Pastor Kahlbauch will comfort my parents. Old Sonnenstich will quote precedents from history. I don't suppose I'll get a gravestone. I would have quite liked a pure white column on a polished black granite slab. Not that I shall miss it, thank God. Memorials are for the living.

So many people to say my farewells to! It would take me a

year even to think through the list. Anyway, main thing is not to cry any more. It's good that I can look back on it all without any bitter feelings. All those happy evenings with Melchior. Under the willows by the river. Up at the forester's lodge. Out on the highway with the five lime trees. On the ancient mound among the Runenberg ruins, hidden away. When the moment comes, I'll think as hard as I can about whipped cream. Whipped cream could never hold you back. It constipates you but has a nice aftertaste. Human beings aren't as bad as I imagined them. I never met one person who wasn't trying to do their very best. I even pitied some – for the trouble I gave them.

So now I'm approaching the altar like that youth in ancient Etruria whose death-rattle was the sign that guaranteed his brother's good fortune. I feel the strange thrills of deliverance – they come one by one, like the dishes of a supper banquet – and a choking sadness – that my fate has been what it has been. Life turned its back on me. In the distance I see grave, friendly faces, welcoming. Once again the headless queen. The headless queen! My consolation! Her soft arms waiting for me. Your laws are valid only for those who cannot take responsibility for their own lives. I have my free pass here. When the chrysalis cracks open, out creeps the butterfly. We are no longer lost in the deceptive picture. The mad game with illusion is not worth playing. The mist has lifted. Life is a matter of taste. You take it. Or you leave it.

Enter Ilse.

Ilse What have you lost?

Moritz Ilse!

Ilse What are you looking for?

Moritz Why did you give me such a fright?

44

Ilse What are you looking for? What have you lost?

Moritz Why did you scare me like that? Look, you've made me shake.

Ilse I've just come from town. I'm going home.

Moritz I don't know what I've lost.

Ilse Why look for it then?

Moritz Oh, Christ! Christ!

Ilse I haven't been home for four days.

Moritz Sneaking up on me like that – like a cat after a mouse.

Ilse It's because I'm in my dancing slippers – so quiet. Mother's going to get a shock too, when she sees me. Come with me as far as our house.

Moritz Where have you been prowling?

Ilse In the Phallopia.

Moritz The Phallopia!

Ilse At Nohl's, at Fehrendorf's, Padinsky's, Lenz's, at Rank's, at Spuhler's – Name who you like – ting-a-ling-a-ling – and up I pop.

Moritz Do they paint you?

Ilse Fehrendorf's painting me as a saint standing on top of a Corinthian column. That Fehrendorf is completely off his rocker. I trod on a tube of his paint. So he cleans his brush in my hair. I give him one smack to make his eyes jump. So he rams his palette into my face. I kick over his easel and he lashes out at me with his maulstick, chases me all round the studio, over the divan, the tables, the chairs – everything goes flying. I grab a big sketch of his from behind the stove. 'Control yourself,' I tell him, 'or I'll rip

45

this to bits.' So we make a truce and finally he kisses me, and I mean kisses me, kisses me right off my feet.

Moritz Where do you sleep when you stay in town?

Ilse Last night at Nohl's. Night before at Bojokewitsch's. Sunday with Oikonomopulos. It was champagne at Padinsky's. Valabregez sold his 'Plague-stricken Man'. Adolar drank out of an ashtray. Lenz sang 'She murdered her baby' and Adolar went berserk on the guitar. Nobody could stop him. I was so drunk they had to carry me to bed. Still at school, Moritz?

Moritz No, no. I've left. I'm leaving this term.

Ilse At last! Once you start earning your living, the days just flash by. Remember when we played at robbers, Wendla Bergman, you and me and the others, and how everybody used to come round to our house in the evening and drink fresh goat's milk still warm. What's Wendla doing these days? I saw her the other day staring at the floods. And Melchi Gabor? Still brooding and pondering. We used to stand opposite each other in singing lessons.

Moritz He's a philosopher.

Ilse Wendla came over to our house and brought some jam. I'd been sitting all day for Isidor Landauer. He wants me for his 'Madonna and the Infant Christ'. That man's such a scoundrel. And disgusting as well. Really revolting. He just rolls wherever the wind happens to blow him. Are you hungover?

Moritz Last night we overdid it a little bit. We spent the whole night drinking as if our lives depended on it. It was five in the morning before I staggered home.

Ilse Well, you show it. Any girls there?

Moritz Arabella – the barmaid. She's a Spaniard –

Andalusian. The landlord just left her with us, the whole night.

Ilse Well, you certainly do show it. I don't know what a hangover is. Last carnival I never got to bed or changed my clothes for three days and three nights. From the ball to the café, the Bellavista at midday, cabaret in the evening, then back to the ball. Lena was there, and Viola – remember the fat girl? Then on the third night Heinrich found me.

Moritz Was he looking for you?

Ilse He tripped over my arm. I was flat out unconscious in the snow on the street. He took me back to his place. I was there two weeks – what a ghastly fortnight that was! Mornings I had to swan about his apartment in his Persian bathrobe. Evenings it was his little black pageboy outfit. White lace at the throat, the wrists and the knees. Every day he'd photograph me in some exotic pose – Ariadne draped over the back of a sofa, or as Leda or Ganymede. Once down on all fours as a female Nebuchadnezzar. All the time he was ranting on about killing, shooting, suicide, gas. Then he'd jump up at three a.m. and come back to bed with a pistol, load it and stick it into my breast. 'Blink once,' he'd say, 'and I'll blast you wide open.' And he would have too, Moritz. He was quite capable, believe me. Then he'd put the thing in his mouth as if it were a blow-pipe. All to rouse my instinct of self-preservation. And then – ugh! The bullet would have gone straight through my backbone.

Moritz Is this man still alive?

Ilse How should I know? Directly over his bed, in the ceiling, was a mirror. It made his tiny den seem to go straight up – like a tower, and very bright, like an opera house. You saw yourself hanging there in the heavens,

47

face downwards. Every night I had the most horrible nightmares. Then I would lie awake just gritting my teeth to make the hours pass – please God, make it morning soon. Good night, Ilse. When you are asleep, do you know, my darling, you are beautiful enough to murder.

Moritz And is he still alive?

Ilse I pray to God he's dead. One day while he was out for his absinthe, I slipped his coat on and got away down the street. Carnival time was long past and the police picked me up. So it's what am I doing in a man's coat and straight off to the police station. Then in came Nohl, Fehrendorf, Padinsky, Spuhler, Oikonomopulos, the whole Phallopia, and they bailed me out. They took me off to Adolar's in a cab. So ever since I've stuck with them. Fehrendorf is a baboon. Nohl is an arsehole. Bojokewitsch is a blockhead. Boison has no principles whatever. And Oikonomopulos is a clown. But I love them all and wouldn't hook up with anybody else, even if the rest of the world were nothing but angels and billionaires.

Moritz I've got to get back, Ilse.

Ilse Come as far as our house.

Moritz Why? What for?

Ilse Come and drink some fresh warm goat's milk. And I'll singe your curls. And I'll hang a little bell around your neck. And we still have a rocking horse you can play with.

Moritz I have to get back. I've still got the Sassanids, the Sermon on the Mount and the parallelepipedon on my conscience – all for tomorrow. Good night, Ilse.

Ilse Sweet dreams! Do you ever go down to the old wigwam where Melchi Gabor buried my tomahawk? Brrr! By the time any of you boys are ready for it, I'll be on the scrap-heap. (*She goes.*)

48

Moritz One word was all it needed. Ilse! Ilse! She seems to be out of hearing, thank God.

Anyway, I'm not in the mood. For that sort of thing your head needs to feel free and your heart happy.

I'll tell them the whole ceiling was a crystal mirror. I broke and trained a wild filly. Made her prance across the room in long black fishnet stockings and black patent high-heeled boots, long black suede gloves, a black velvet band round her neck with a big pearl in it – and in a fit of madness I smothered her with a pillow. When they talk about passion, I'll smile. I'll SCREAM – I SHALL SCREAM – ILSE – TO BE YOU, IF ONLY I COULD BE YOU. PHALLOPIA! – BLACKNESS! – NOTHINGNESS! IT DRAINS MY STRENGTH! THIS CHILD OF BLESSED GOOD FORTUNE, THIS DAZZLING CREATURE. THIS BLISSFUL TEMPTRESS THAT CROSSES MY HORRIBLE PATH – OH! OH!

Among riverbank rushes.

It looks as if instinct has led me back to my grassy bank. These mallows have grown since yesterday. The view out through the willows, though, that's the same. Unchanged. The river moves like molten lead. One thing I must not forget. (*Burns Frau Gabor's letter.*) See how the flame eats it. Here and there, – frittering away – sparking off into nothing – souls – shooting stars! Before I lit the match I could see the meadows and a band of light along the horizon. Everything's suddenly quite dark. I shan't go home now, no, never again.

Act Three

SCENE ONE

In the staff room. Assembled teachers and Habebald the caretaker.

Sonnenstich Do any of you gentlemen have any further remarks to make?

Gentlemen, if we were to ignore the need for prompt action in applying to the relevant department of the Ministry of Education for the expulsion of this criminally guilty pupil of ours, we could be accused of ignoring arguments that are quite simply irrefutable. Such action cannot be avoided if we are not to be seen to condone this outbreak of evil that has occurred. It cannot be avoided if we are to defend this establishment against similar calamities in the future. It cannot be avoided if this criminally guilty boy is not to escape undisciplined and unaware of the true gravity of his crime. And it cannot be avoided if he is to be made fully conscious of his responsibility for the corrupting influence he has had on his fellow students. Even more important, such action cannot be avoided if we are to extirpate this malignant influence from our classrooms. But most important of all – and here the reasons compelling us to action carry this whole issue beyond argument – such action is literally forced upon us unless we are to abandon our school to the epidemic of suicides now sweeping through many other schools like it, an epidemic which has up to now overwhelmed all efforts to restrain pupils within those civilized conditions of existence that are created by the assiduous cultivation of a noble and refined character.

Do any of you gentlemen have any further remarks to make?

Knuppeldick Without seeming to be impatient, I cannot suppress my conviction that it is about time somebody opened a window in here.

Zungenschlag The atmosph-ph-ph-phere in here is like that in the deep ca-ca-ca-catacombs of Egypt, or in what used to be the-the old ca-ca-ca-courtroom in Wetzlar.

Sonnenstich Habebald.

Habebald At your command, Herr Sonnenstich.

Sonnenstich Open a window. Fortunately, there is air in plenty outside. Now, has anybody anything to add to what has been said?

Fliegentod I have no desire to oppose my colleagues if they wish to have a window open. But may I make one request: that it should not be the window directly behind the back of my neck.

Sonnenstich Open the other window then. Do any of you gentlemen have any further remarks to make?

Hungergurt I would not wish to seem to be contradicting anyone, but might I remind those present that the other window has been bricked up since the autumn holidays last year.

Sonnenstich Habebald!

Habebald At your command, Herr Sonnenstich.

Sonnenstich Let the other window stay closed. I see that this matter will be settled only by the democratic method. Gentlemen, we seem to have only one window that is relevant to the matter in hand. May I ask all who are in favour of opening this window to stand up. One, two, three. One, two, three, Habebald.

Habebald At your command, Herr Sonnenstich.

Sonnenstich Leave the other window closed. To be quite frank, the atmosphere in here seems to me perfectly satisfactory.

Do any of you gentlemen have any further remarks to make?

Gentlemen, once again: if we fail to apply for this boy's expulsion it will mean only one thing to the education authorities. They will hold us responsible for the whole disastrous affair. You may not be aware, but the consequences of that could well be serious. Of the various schools that have been hit by the suicide epidemic, those schools in which twenty-five per cent of the pupils have succumbed have been suspended – by the education authority. As the custodians of this establishment, obviously our first duty must be to protect it from such a catastrophe. It grieves me deeply that this criminally guilty boy's qualifications in other respects cannot be brought in as mitigating circumstances. The plight of the boy might of itself seem to deserve a more lenient decision, but in the larger situation, where the very survival of our school is in question, such a point of view would be irrational and quite impossible to justify. We find ourselves, therefore, compelled to pronounce judgement on this boy's guilt, lest we, the innocent, find ourselves judged. Habebald!

Habebald At your command, Herr Sonnenstich.

Sonnenstich Bring him up.

Zungenschlag If the prevailing atmosph-ph-ph-phere in this chamber should be ca-ca-ca-considered, on average, to l-l-leave little or n-nothing to be desired, then may I propose that during the summer holiday the other window be bricked up a-a-a-as-as-as well.

Fliegentod If our esteemed colleague Zungenschlag finds the ventilation of our little sanctum so inadequate, may I propose that our esteemed colleague Zungenschlag arranges to have a small ventilator installed in his brain.

Zungenschlag That is perfectly ou-ou-ou-outrageous. Have I to tolerate such boo-boo-boo-boorishness? All my fa-fa-fac-cu-cu-faculties are as-as-as-as sound as yours, thank you very much.

Sonnenstich I really must ask our esteemed colleagues Fliegentod and Zungenschlag to preserve some measure of decorum. The culprit is here.

Habebald leads in Melchior.

Approach the table. After Councillor Steifel, the devastated father, had been informed of his son Moritz's appalling act, he searched through the boy's personal effects in the hope of finding some clue to explain such a repellent crime. It so happened that he did find something – exactly where need not detain us. A manuscript – a very strange document which, without providing sufficient motivation for the atrocity itself, nevertheless does, unfortunately, more than account for the state of moral depravity which, we believe, was decisive, without any doubt, in the execution of the criminal act. The document in question comprises a twenty-page discourse entitled 'Sexual Reproduction'. It is cast in the form of a philosophical dialogue, in the manner of Plato, and is embellished throughout with almost life-size drawings illustrating the most revolting obscenities, utterly shameless material that would satisfy, one imagines, the basest prurient appetites of the most degenerate, debauched, bestial pervert –

Melchior I will –

Sonnenstich You will remain silent! Having received this object from the distressed Herr Steifel, we gave him our word that we would leave no stone unturned to bring the author to light. It was then a simple matter to compare the handwriting with that of all this deceased malefactor's fellow pupils. The entire teaching staff gave a unanimous verdict, which was supported without reservation, after a thorough scrutiny, by our esteemed expert instructor in calligraphy. The handwriting is yours.

Melchior I will –

Sonnenstich You will remain silent! Despite the absolute proof of this identification, we believe we should defer the next three steps until the suspect has been rigorously examined concerning the enormity with which he is charged – in other words, the immoral act he perpetrated which proved tantamount to incitement to suicide.

Melchior I will –

Sonnenstich You will listen. Precisely formulated questions will now be put to you. You will answer each one with an unequivocal 'yes' or'no'. Habebald!

Habebald At your command, Herr Sonnenstich.

Sonnenstich Bring the papers. I call upon Professor Fliegentod, as secretary, to minute our proceedings from this point with extreme care, word for word if possible.

(*To Melchior*) Now, do you recognize this handwriting?

Melchior Yes.

Sonnenstich Are you familiar with the contents of this manuscript?

Melchior Yes.

Sonnenstich Is this your handwriting?

Melchior Yes.

Sonnenstich Are you the author of this obscene piece of work?

Melchior Yes. But I call upon you, Headmaster, to point out one single obscenity.

Sonnenstich You will restrict your answers to 'yes' or 'no'.

Melchior Sir, I have written nothing but the simple straightforward facts, familiar to you and to every adult.

Sonnenstich Insolent – !

Melchior I call on you, Sir, to show me one example where my account contradicts or misrepresents our accepted adult behaviour.

Sonnenstich Are you trying to make a fool of me too, Gabor? You are a barbarian! Habebald!

Melchior I have –

Sonnenstich You have as little respect for the dignity of these assembled representatives of our educational system as you do for those sacred instincts of modesty and decorum that are rooted in the moral order of the world. Habebald!

Habebald At your command, Herr Sonnenstich.

Sonnenstich This is a manual of abominations, it is Langenscheidt's agglutinative Esperanto in three hours!

Melchior I call upon –

Sonnenstich I call upon Herr Fliegentod to close the minutes.

Melchior I will –

Sonnenstich You will be silent! Habebald.

Habebald At your command, Herr Sonnenstich.

Sonnenstich Take him down.

SCENE TWO

Cemetery in pouring rain. Mourners at graveside.

Pastor Kahlbauch For he who rejects the grace with which the Eternal Father has blessed man that is born in sin, he shall die the death of the spirit. He who honours not God and in his wilful fleshly denial of God's grace lives in and serves evil, he shall die the death of the body. But he who heedlessly casts aside the cross that the all-merciful has laid upon him for his sins, verily, verily I say unto you, he shall die the death everlasting. (*Earth into the grave.*) For as surely as this person died the threefold death, so surely shall God lead his righteous faithful into heavenly bliss and life everlasting.

Herr Steifel (*earth into the grave*) That boy was no son of mine. I knew it the day he was born. I could never take to him.

Sonnenstich (*earth into the grave*) As the most unimaginable violation of the moral code, suicide is at the same time the strongest possible confirmation of its existence. In so far as the victim relieves the moral code from the onus of passing judgement, he simultaneously proves how indispensable that moral code is.

Knockenbruch (*earth into the grave*) Delinquent, defective, depraved, despicable, detestable, degenerate –

Probst (*earth into the grave*) Even if I heard it from my own dear mother, I would never have believed a child could act so vindictively against its own parents.

Ziegenmelker (*earth into the grave*) To inflict this shame on his father – a man totally driven for the last fourteen years from morn till night by his concern for his son's future.

Pastor Kahlbauch (*shaking Steifel's hand*) For them that love God, all things are for the best. Now you must think of the boy's unhappy mother. You must make up her loss by redoubling your love to her.

Sonnenstich (*shaking Steifel's hand*) In any event, he would almost certainly have been dropped from the higher class.

Knockenbruch (*shaking Steifel's hand*) Even if he'd been allowed to go up this time, he would quite definitely have failed next spring.

Probst (*shaking Steifel's hand*) Your duty now is to keep things in proportion. Remember – put yourself first. You are the father and head of a family.

Ziegenmelker (*shaking Steifel's hand*) If you need anyone, I'm here. Trust yourself to my guidance. Such God-awful weather – goes straight through the guts. What's needed now is a good strong drink and pretty soon too, if the old heart's to bear up under all this.

Herr Steifel He was no son of mine. I always knew it –

They go. Rain ceases.

Rilow (*earth into the grave*) Rest in peace, my fine friend. Give my salutations to all those immortal beauties of my never-to-be-forgotten sacrifices. And put in a word for me to the dear Lord – you poor bloody simpleton. All your grave needs now is a scarecrow – to commemorate your angelic naïvety.

Ernst Have they found the pistol?

Otto No point looking for anything like that.

Georg Did you see him, Otto?

Rilow They covered him with a sheet. The whole thing was wrapped up. Who did see him?

Georg Was his tongue hanging out?

Otto His eyes were – lolling right out. That's why they covered him.

Ernst Oh, God, how disgusting!

Rilow Are you sure he hanged himself?

Georg They say the whole head was just gone.

Otto Rubbish! I handled the actual rope he used. I've never seen anybody hanged who didn't have to be covered up.

Ernst Well, what a horrible goodbye he's given us all.

Rilow Oh, what the hell! Hanging's said to have its compensations.

Otto He owes me five marks. We had a bet. He bet me he'd keep his place in the class.

Rilow Yes, and you said he was talking out of the top of his head. It's your fault he's down there now.

Otto Don't be stupid! I had to slog the whole night too. If he'd mastered his Greek, he needn't have hanged himself.

Ernst Have you done the essay, Otto?

Otto I think I've got my introduction.

Ernst I can't think even how to begin. Let alone what to follow it with.

Georg Weren't you there when old Affenschmalz set the assignment?

Rilow I'll find something in Aristotle on ethics.

Ernst I'm going to dig around in the encyclopedia.

Otto Have you done the Virgil for tomorrow?

Boys go. Martha and Ilse.

Ilse Hurry up. The grave-diggers are coming to fill in the grave.

Martha Shouldn't we wait, Ilse?

Ilse Why? We can bring fresh ones. Then go on bringing more fresh ones. There's plenty growing.

Martha Yes, you're right.

They throw fresh flowers into the grave.

I'll dig up our roses. I might as well do something to be beaten for. They'll grow beautifully here.

Ilse Then every time I pass I'll water them. I'll bring forget-me-nots from over by the stream, and irises from home.

Martha It's going to look heavenly. Heavenly!

Ilse I'd only just got across the bridge when I heard the shot.

Martha How awful.

Ilse And I know why he did it, Martha.

Martha What did he tell you?

Ilse Parallelepipedon. Keep that to yourself.

Martha I will. Parallelepipedon!

Ilse And here's the pistol.

Martha Oh, Ilse – so that's why nobody could find it.

Ilse When I came past next morning, I simply took it out of his hand.

Martha Oh, give it to me. Oh, Ilse, please let me have it.

Ilse No, it's my souvenir of him.

Martha Ilse, is it true he's lying down there without a head?

Ilse He must have loaded this thing with water. The mallows were all draped with blood. His brains were hanging from the willows.

SCENE THREE

Herr and Frau Gabor.

Frau Gabor They needed a scapegoat. They couldn't let all these accusations flying everywhere end up sticking to them, could they? My son was a godsend. He had the luck to fall in their path at just the right moment. And those unscrupulous old pedants pounced on him. And now I, his own mother, am supposed to complete their dirty work and finish him off. Well, God forbid.

Herr Gabor For fourteen years I have observed your enlightened methods for bringing up children and all this time I have kept silent. Your ideas have been quite markedly the reverse of mine. My own belief has never faltered: a child is not a toy. A child merits our gravest attention. But then I persuaded myself that if the seriousness and severity of my ideas could be replaced successfully by the spirit and charm of yours, then the latter might in the long run turn out to be no bad thing. Fanny, I do not blame you. But when I try to rectify the damage that you and I have done to the boy, do not bar my way.

Frau Gabor I shall bar your way till you have to step over my dead body. Reformatory would crush my child, it would utterly destroy him. Maybe institutions of that kind can correct a boy naturally given to crime. I wouldn't know. But how could any normal child survive such a place? They'd be turned into criminals – as sure as a plant deprived of light and water will shrivel up. What did I do wrong? I cannot think I did anything wrong. I strove to create nobility of mind and uprightness of character, and I thanked God continually for showing me the way. What has the boy done that's so terrible? I would never dream of making excuses for him – but just because his headmaster has decided to expel him from school doesn't automatically mean he's guilty. And even if he were, hasn't the poor child more than paid for it already? Perhaps you are wiser than I am. Theoretically your attitude might be considered correct. But I can't let my only child be broken and crushed and torn to pieces in this way.

Herr Gabor My dear, it is no longer in our hands. It was a risk we took as parents – together with our happiness. This possibility was there from the very start. Those who can't make the march must be left at the wayside. And if this thing was inevitable – then in the final reckoning it is not the worst thing for it to have arrived early. But as long as reason points out a clear direction, it is our duty to guide the waverer through his dark moment.

You say Melchior is not to blame for being expelled from school. If he had not been expelled, that would not have been his fault either. You are altogether too superficial. You see only innocent-minded exploration, but in fact we are looking at a fundamental deformity of character. In a case of this kind, you women are simply not qualified to judge. Whoever wrote what he wrote in that paper must be rotten to the very core. The very essence of his being is corrupt. Any vestigial trace of morality would have made such a flagrant act impossible. None of us is a saint. Everyone deviates at times from the straight and narrow. But what he did is the symptom of a deeper sickness. No, my dear, this was no transgression for curiosity's sake. It exemplifies with quite shattering clarity an ingrained predisposition, an obsessive fascination with what is immoral for no other reason than that it is immoral. His manuscript displays that abnormal degree of moral depravity for which we lawyers have a term – 'moral insanity'. Whether anything can be done for his condition, I truly cannot say. But as the parents of the boy in question, if we want to retain one glimmer of hope for ourselves, and above all to retain our own absolute purity of conscience, we must address ourselves seriously to the task and act swiftly. No more argument, Fanny. I'm only too aware how hard this is going to be for you. I know how you idolize him, and that is understandable. He brings to expression something of your own highly original nature. But I must ask you now, be stronger than yourself. For once in your life, in our son's terrible crisis, be selfless.

Frau Gabor Oh, God! How is all that to be answered! Only a man could speak like that. Only a man could be such a blind slave to somebody else's pronouncements. It takes a man to bow down to empty words and close his eyes to the huge obvious fact. I saw very early that Melchior is unusually responsive to everything around him, unusually sensitive, and for that reason, it is true, I have always been especially careful with him, as you have observed. But nobody can anticipate accidents. Tomorrow a tile off a roof could land on your head and knock you unconscious. But then imagine if some friend of yours came along – imagine if your own father came along – and instead of tending your wound simply stamped on your head. I won't let my child be murdered while I stand by and watch. How could a mother do that? It's unthinkable! And what is so inhumanly dreadful about what he wrote anyway? The very fact that he could write it proves beyond any doubt just how naïve he really is, how childishly unaware of how it appears to adults. How pure and harmless he is. Does it require profound insight into human nature to see that? You'd need the soul of a bureaucrat, operated entirely by rules and statistics, with no experience of life whatsoever, to find moral corruption there. Say what you like. But if you put Melchior in the Reformatory I shall divorce you. Then I shall look somewhere else for a way to save him, and somewhere in this world I shall find it.

Herr Gabor You will have to accept what is happening, Fanny. If not today, then tomorrow. Overcoming our misfortunes is not easy, not for anyone. My dear, whenever the burden becomes too much for you, whenever your courage begins to fail, I shall be there at your side, to support you with all my strength. What I see of the future is already dark enough. If I were to lose you, the disaster would be complete.

Frau Gabor I shall never see him again. I shall never see him again. The degradation will crush him. He'll never be able to bear the filth. He'll lose his last bit of self-respect. And he'll have that hideous example of Moritz Steifel – night and day, hanging in front of him. If ever I do see him again – oh, God, God, his happy heart, like a spring day, his bright laughter – everything! Everything! – That boyish fierce determination to fight for what is right and good – Oh, like a dawn sky without one stain, how I cherished and nursed it, so clear and pure in his soul, the treasure of my life! – Blame me! Make me pay! Do what you like with me! The guilt's all mine! But keep your terrible hands off my child.

Herr Gabor He has committed a crime.

Frau Gabor He has not committed a crime.

Herr Gabor He has committed a crime. I know your love for him is infinite, and I would have done anything to spare you from having to face this fact. Melchior has committed a crime.

This morning a woman came to see me. She was in such a state she could hardly speak. She gave me this letter, which had been sent to her fourteen-year-old daughter. She had opened it out of thoughtless curiosity. The girl wasn't at home. In this letter, Melchior begs the girl's forgiveness for what he did to her – for the sin he committed, etc. etc. He assures her he will take responsibility for everything. And she should not feel ashamed – even if there are consequences that cannot be hidden. He's already searching high and low for help – his expulsion from school has made things easier in that respect. His original lapse may yet turn out to be her greatest happiness – and so on, a long rigmarole of similar nonsense.

Frau Gabor Impossible!

Herr Gabor Of course it is. The letter's a forgery. The whole thing's made up. News of his expulsion has spread all over town and somebody's trying to turn it to profit. I haven't yet confronted the boy with it, but please, take a look at the handwriting.

Frau Gabor Outrageous! Disgusting! Shameless!

Herr Gabor I'm afraid it is just that.

Frau Gabor No, no – never.

Herr Gabor This makes our decision easier. The woman was wringing her hands and asking me what she ought to do. Keep your daughter out of haylofts, I told her. Luckily she left the letter with me. If we send him to some other school, away from parental supervision, another three weeks and he'll be giving a repeat performance. Expelled again. And that happy heart of his so full of pure dawn light like a spring day will soon be finding this kind of behaviour quite congenial. Fanny, what in God's name am I to do with the boy?

Frau Gabor Send him to the Reformatory.

Herr Gabor To the – ?

Frau Gabor To the Reformatory.

Herr Gabor He will find there what he was so mistakenly denied here at home: iron discipline, principles, and a moral order that cannot under any circumstances be challenged or stood on its head. And you are quite wrong to suppose that the Reformatory is such a benighted place. Everything is done to develop a Christian mentality and a Christian sensibility. That is the model there. Without any alternative. The boy will learn to want what is good rather than what titillates his curiosity. And his behaviour will be decided by the rules rather than by his own natural instincts. Half an hour ago I heard from my brother. He fully confirmed what the woman told me. Melchior has confided in him and asked for two hundred marks to escape to England.

Frau Gabor Oh, God have mercy!

SCENE FOUR

In the Reformatory.

Diethelm Here's twenty pfennings.

Reinhold What about it?

Diethelm I put this on the floor. Now make a ring. Whoever hits it, gets it.

Ruprecht Melchior, come on.

Melchior No thanks.

Helmuth Mummy won't let him.

Gaston Anyway he can't any more, he's here trying to recover.

Melchior It's not such a bright idea, keeping myself apart. They all watch me. I shall have to join in – or everything goes to hell! Prison makes them suicidal. If I end up with my neck broken, that's fine. And if I get out in one piece, well that's fine too. So I can't really lose. I can make a friend of Ruprecht, and he knows the ropes in here. I'll amuse him with the story of Judah's daughter-in-law, Tamar. Lot and his daughters. Queen Vashti. Abishag and Shulamite. He has the most smashed-up face in the whole bunch.

Ruprecht I'm coming.

Helmuth Me too.

Gaston Day after tomorrow maybe.

Helmuth Soon! Now! Oh, God, God!

All *Summa! Summa cum laude!*

Ruprecht Thanks very much.

Helmuth Give it here, you bastard.

Ruprecht Bastard yourself.

Helmuth Jailbird.

Ruprecht There! (*Hits him, runs.*)

Helmuth I'll pulp him!

Rest After him! Hunt him down! Get him!

All run out. Melchior on his own.

Melchior The lightning conductor's earthing wire comes
down here. You need to wrap a handkerchief round it.
Whenever I think of her, the blood pounds into my skull.
And Moritz – he's a ton of lead in my feet. I'll get a job
with a newspaper, paid by the hundred words, churn the
stuff out – trashy stories – current affairs – local gossip –
moral problems – medical titbits – it's not easy to die of
hunger these days. Soup kitchens, free meals for the down
and out. This place is sixty feet high and the façade's
coming away from the bricks. It's certain she hates me. She
hates me because I've robbed her of her freedom.
Whatever I do, whatever I try to make of it – the rape
stays a rape. The only hope – is time. As the years pass– –
she'll gradually – One week from now on is the new
moon. Tomorrow I'll grease the hinges. Saturday is the
very latest I must know who's got the key. In prayers on
Sunday evening I'll fake a cataleptic fit – I only pray to
God nobody else falls really sick. It's all as clear in my
head as if I'd already done it. Out I went, over the
windowsill, no problem – one swing and grabbed the
cable. You have to wrap a handkerchief round it. Here
comes the Grand Inquisitor. (*Exits.*)

Dr Prokrustes and locksmith.

Dr Prokrustes These windows are on the second floor and
directly below are dense beds of stinging nettles. But what
do these hardened thugs care about a few stings? Last
winter one climbed out through a skylight – so then we
had all the trouble of gathering him up, carting him off
and burying him.

Locksmith Well, Sir, it looks to me like a wrought-iron-
grille job.

Dr Prokrustes Exactly. Wrought iron. And since it can't be let in to the surrounding bricks, bolt it right through the wall.

SCENE FIVE

Wendla's bedroom. Wendla in bed.

Dr Brausepulver What's your age?

Wendla Fourteen and a half.

Dr Brausepulver I've been prescribing these Blaud's tablets now for fifteen years. In the majority of cases, the patient's condition improves in a way that can only be described as startling. Much to be preferred, I think, to cod liver oil and iron tonics. Start with three or four pills a day and increase the number as rapidly as you find you can tolerate the strengthening dose. To give you some idea: I told Fraülein Elfriede, the Baroness von Witzleben, to take one extra tablet every third day. She listened too anxiously, as patients do, and therefore took three extra tablets every day. And what was the result? Within three weeks she could accompany her mother to Pyrmont for after-care. I absolve you from any special diet and you have no need to tire yourself out with long walks. But you must promise me one thing, dear child, in return. You must make all your movements as vigorous as possible, and as your appetite improves, do not be shy about asking for extra helpings. That's most important. The palpitations will soon go, together with the headaches, the chills, the giddiness, not to mention these fearful difficulties with the digestion. Within one week of starting her treatment, Fraülein Elfriede, the Baroness von Witzleben, was eating one whole roasted chicken and a heap of new potatoes in their skins – for breakfast!

Frau Bergman Can I offer you a glass of wine, Doctor?

Dr Brausepulver Thank you, but no, my dear Frau Bergman. I must not. My carriage is waiting. Now don't let this business get on top of you. In a few weeks' time, our pretty little patient will be frisky as a gazelle. Good day, Frau Bergman. Good day, my dear child. Good day, ladies, good day.

Frau Bergman shows him out.

Ina (*at the window*) Your plane tree's suddenly full of colour again. Can you see it from your pillow? Yet it's so brief, all that beauty. When you see it come like that, and know it's only come to go, one can hardly call it a bringer of joy, can one? I must go. My husband's waiting for me in front of the post office and I have to get to the dressmaker's first. It will be Muccki's first pair of trousers and I'm having a new woolly winter outfit made for Karl.

Wendla I have waves of the most wonderful sensation – endless joy. I never knew it was possible to feel so much. I want to walk out over the river meadows, just as the sun's going down, find primroses along the banks, and simply sit there, watching the river and dreaming – Then I have an attack of toothache and feel I'm going to die within twenty-four hours. I'm hot and cold, sweating and shivering, then everything goes black and that monster comes flying in. And every time I open my eyes, I see my mother sobbing. Oh, Ina, it's all so painful. I couldn't begin to tell you.

Ina Let me arrange your pillows.

Frau Bergman (*entering*) The doctor says your waves of nausea will pass and then, if you're very careful, you can get up. I think it would be better for you to get up soon too, Wendla.

Ina Next time I see you, I expect you'll be dashing about the house again. Goodbye, Mother. I must get to that dressmaker. God bless, Wendla. (*Kisses her.*) Get better now.

Wendla Farewell, Ina. And next time you come, bring some primroses. Say hello to your boys for me. Adieu.

Exit Ina.

What else did the doctor say when he was outside there with you, Mother?

Frau Bergman Nothing. He only mentioned that Fräulein von Witzleben, also, had a tendency to faint. That's usual in cases of anaemia.

Wendla He told you I had anaemia?

Frau Bergman You're to drink milk and eat plenty of meat and fruit as your appetite improves.

Wendla Mother, whatever I have is not anaemia.

Frau Bergman You are anaemic, Wendla. Please don't get agitated, child. You simply have anaemia.

Wendla No, Mother, I haven't. I know. It isn't anaemia. It's dropsy –

Frau Bergman Wendla, the doctor said you have anaemia. You're anaemic. Now please do not get so excited, girl. It is easy to cure.

Wendla Oh, no, it isn't. It can't be cured. I've got dropsy and I have to die. I know it. Oh, Mother, Mother, I'm going to die.

Frau Bergman You do not have to die, my child! You must not die. Oh, God have mercy! Wendla, you are not going to die.

Wendla Then why are you crying like that, Mother?

Frau Bergman You're not going to die. You haven't got

dropsy. You're going to have a baby, Wendla. You're having a baby. Oh, how could you do this to us?

Wendla I haven't done anything to you.

Frau Bergman You can't deny it. I know what's gone on, Wendla. I know everything. But I couldn't speak about it. Oh, Wendla, my Wendla!

Wendla But that's impossible, Mother. It's impossible. I'm not married.

Frau Bergman God in heaven, help us – don't you see, girl, that's the whole point. You are not married. That's what's so terrible. Wendla! Wendla! Wendla! Don't you see what you've done?

Wendla No, I don't see. We were lying in the hay. But I've never loved anybody in the world except you, Mother.

Frau Bergman Oh, my precious darling child!

Wendla Why didn't you tell me things, Mother?

Frau Bergman Oh, my child, let's not tear each other's hearts any worse. There. We must try to be calm. Don't despair, my darling. How can one tell such things to a fourteen-year-old girl? I would have expected the sun to go dark sooner than – I brought you up exactly as I was brought up by my own mother. We have to trust in the dear Lord, Wendla. We must pray for mercy and do our duty. Besides, so far nothing has happened, nothing at all, not really. If we're resolute and courageous, God will not abandon us. Be brave, Wendla, you must be brave. You sit with your hands folded, gazing out of the window, because everything has always turned out so well, then suddenly – in flies something that almost shatters the heart in your chest and – Why are you trembling?

Wendla I heard a knock at the door.

Frau Bergman I heard nothing. (*She goes to the door.*)

Wendla I heard it. Very clear. Who's there?

Frau Bergman Nobody. It's only old Mother Schmidt from Gartenstrasse. You're right on time, Mother Schmidt.

SCENE SIX

Grape-picking. Rilow and Robel sprawl side by side.

Robel I've overdone it.

Rilow No need to droop. Let a few minutes go by. They'll go by anyway.

Robel You see them hanging so close in their fat globes – and you're done in. Tomorrow they'll all have gone into the wine press.

Rilow This kind of exhaustion reminds me of hunger. I don't know which is worse.

Robel I've had it for today.

Rilow Just one more plump cluster of muscatel grapes.

Robel I can't move.

Rilow I can bend this branch down, and swing it to and fro from my mouth to your mouth and back again. We don't need to move. And when we've bitten off every grape, we let the branch go.

Robel Amazing how you can be lying exhausted and then a single decision fills you with energy again.

Rilow You can add that glowing sky, those evening bells in the distance. I don't suppose my future holds much that will be better than this.

Robel Sometimes I see myself as a vicar, very dignified and respected, with a cosy little wife, a comfortable library and a string of small honours. I contemplate creation for six days and talk about it on the seventh. As I walk along, schoolboys and schoolgirls come up to shake my hand and bow, their heels together. Back in the vicarage, there's steaming coffee, freshly baked cake brought into the parlour, girls coming in through the back door with their pinafores full of apples. Can you imagine anything more beautiful?

Rilow Eyes half-closed, lips half-open, Turkish draperies. It's sentimentality that I can't stand. Grown-ups pull their long, solemn, important faces to cover their own stupidity. Among themselves, they call each other imbeciles and fools, just as we do. I've seen through all that. When I'm a millionaire, I'll set up a memorial to God Almighty. Just think of the future as a milk pudding with cinnamon and sugar. Some knock it over and burst into tears. Some mix it all up, then struggle to swallow the whole lot. But why not just skim off a little of the cream? Or do you think that kind of ingenuity is beyond us?

Robel Yes, let's skim off a little of the cream!

Rilow Chuck the rest to the hens. I've pulled my head out of many a noose before now, I can tell you!

Robel Skim the cream, Hanschen. Let's skim the cream. Why are you laughing?

Rilow You're off again!

Robel Somebody has to start.

Rilow In thirty years' time, we'll remember this evening. It will seem unspeakably beautiful.

Robel Everything seems to be just happening of its own accord.

Rilow And why not?

Robel If I were alone now, I might even let a tear roll down.

Rilow This is no time for being weepy. (*Kisses him on the mouth.*)

Robel When I left home, all I was expecting was to have a bit of a talk with you.

Rilow Well, I was lying in wait. Virtue is an impressive uniform – but it needs a special kind of figure. It's not for ordinary men.

Robel It certainly feels outsize on us. If I hadn't met you, Hanschen, I would never have got myself out of my black hole. I've never loved anybody or anything as I love you.

Rilow Let's not be melancholy about it. In thirty years' time we'll laugh at all this, most likely. But everything is so beautiful this evening. The mountain tops glow. The great bunches of grapes weigh down into our mouths. The evening breeze brushes the leaves along the cliff like a teasing caress –

SCENE SEVEN

The cemetery: moonlit night, windy. Melchior jumps down from the wall.

Melchior The pack will never find me here. While they're searching the brothels, I'll get my breath back and take stock. Think what next. Coat ripped to shreds, pockets empty, every living soul ready to point me out and turn me in. When there's light enough, I'll have to find a way through the woods.

That was a cross I knocked over. A night like this, any

74

flowers will be frozen stiff. Bare earth everywhere. The land of the dead.

Climbing through that skylight was nothing to this. I'm not sure I was quite ready for this.

Like the roof of the abyss. Holes in the earth. Everything sinking away in front of me – Why didn't I stay where I was?

Why should she bear the punishment for what was my crime? Why don't I bear it? That's why they call providence inscrutable. I would have broken stones, starved myself –

What keeps me going? Something. One crime drops you through to the next. I'm condemned to the lowest sludge. Too weak even to put an end to it.

But I wasn't evil. I was not evil. I was not evil.

No living person wandering among graves ever felt such envy – to be down among them. Ah, but I haven't the guts. If only I could be insane enough. If only I could go just briefly mad – tonight. The new graves are over there. I should take a look. The wind plays in a different key on each headstone. Dismal symphony! The wreaths disintegrate and bits hang dangling on strings over the faces of stones. Like a forest of scarecrows. On every grave a scarecrow, each one more horrible than the last – faces looming like housefronts, frightening off the devils. That gleaming gold lettering looks very bleak. And that's the weeping willow groaning. Leafy fingers stroking the epitaphs.

And now a praying cherub. And an engraved slab.

The shadow of a cloud. It pours across the heavens. It seems to howl silently. It boils and piles up out of the east, like a vast military campaign. Not a star to be seen.

Evergreen around this one. Evergreen – a girl.

Here rests in God
Wendla Bergman
Born 5 May 1878
died of anaemia
27 October 1892

Blessed are the pure in heart

I killed her. Her murderer – me! No point in crying here. I
must get out. I must get away from this place. Get away –

Moritz (*he comes walking over the graves, his head under
his arm*) Melchior, just a moment! It might be a long time
before we get another opportunity. You have no idea how
totally everything depends on the time and the place.

Melchior Where did you come from?

Moritz Over there by the wall. You knocked my cross
over. They buried me by the wall. Melchior, give me your
hand.

Melchior You are not Moritz Steifel.

Moritz Your hand! You'll thank me before you've
finished. For you, Melchior, nothing will ever again be
easy. But what a rare and happy meeting! I came across on
purpose, just for you –

Melchior Don't you sleep?

Moritz You wouldn't call it sleep. We sit on church
towers, peaks of high gables, anywhere we like –

Melchior You never rest?

Moritz We amuse ourselves. We hang around maypoles
and lonely forest chapels. We hover over any massed
crowds, any mob, public disasters, public gardens,
fairgrounds. Inside people's houses we hide behind the

76

curtains, sometimes in the fireplace. Give me your hand. We stay clear of one another, but we watch everything in the world, and hear everything too. We know that all the works and strivings of mankind are empty folly. And we laugh at it.

Melchior What's the point of that?

Moritz Why should it have a point? We're beyond everything – neither good nor evil can touch us. We float high above earthly existence, each of us quite alone. And we avoid each other because we find each other so boring. None of us owns anything that would grieve us to lose. Joy and despair are equally remote from us. We're simply happy as we are. And there's nothing more to it. To our eyes, the living seem contemptible. We can hardly even feel pity for them. They amuse us. We smile to watch them rushing about in their empty, catastrophic anxiety. And we make our own little observations. Give me your hand. If you would give me your hand, you'd collapse in laughter at the surge of emotion such a simple action would release – you giving me your hand –

Melchior Doesn't that disgust you, isn't that what you despise?

Moritz We're above all that. We smile. I walked among the mourners at my own funeral. I had a really good time! What a comical charade! Melchior, it touched the sublime. My sobbings outdid everybody's. Then I slunk off to the wall there and was nearly sick with laughing. The whole human mess is unbearable – but from our viewpoint, from our all-seeing, all-hearing *inaccessibility*, we laugh at it. I gather they laughed at me, too, before I got up among them.

Melchior I can't say I feel like laughing at myself.

Moritz It is impossible to feel pity for the living. Granted, at one time that's the last thing I could have thought or said. But now it's incomprehensible to me that anybody could be so naïve. Wherever I look, I see through the whole sham – nothing can be hidden. But give me your hand, Melchior. Why are you so reluctant? In one flash you'll be looking down at yourself from far above. And you'll see. Your life is a sin of omission.

Melchior Can the dead forget?

Moritz We can do anything. Give me your hand. We can be sorry for the young, who mistake their helpless frustration for lofty idealism, and for the old, whose arrogant pride makes their hearts so brittle. We can see presidents panicked by a popular song and derelicts in terror of the last judgement. We look under the actor's mask and we watch the poet don his mask in the dark. We see the rich man who owns nothing but his shirt and the greedy capitalist in the pleading beggar. We take note of lovers and observe how hostile they are to each other, deceivers nosing out deception. We listen to parents whose whole purpose is to have children, only so they can shout at them: 'You don't know how lucky you are to have such parents!' And we watch the children go and do the same. We spy on the innocent in their lonely craving for passion, and we eavesdrop on the poor whore quoting Schiller. We can see God and the Devil making fools of themselves as they try to make fools of each other, and we hug to ourselves the unutterable secret – that both are drunk. Melchior – it is the most wonderful feeling, wonderfully tranquil, restful. And all you have to do is give me your little finger. Your hair will be snow white before the opportunity comes your way again.

Melchior If I do this, Moritz, I do it out of pure self-contempt. Here in the world I have become a pariah, a leper. The one thing that could give me courage lies in that grave. I regard myself now as unfit for normal emotions, let alone noble thoughts. I don't see anything that can justify my going on living. Judging myself objectively, there can be no more despicable creature on this earth –

Moritz Then why hold back?

Masked gentleman enters.

Masked Gentleman (*to Melchior*) You are trembling. You are faint with hunger. This is no state of mind for a serious decision. You – go.

Melchior Who are you?

Masked Gentleman In time you will know well enough. I told you to leave us. What are you doing here anyway? And why aren't you wearing your head?

Moritz I shot it off.

Masked Gentleman Stay where you belong. You are done with. Do you understand that? Stop pestering us with your maggoty ghoul-talk. Look at your finger-ends – incredible! Holy God! They're crumbling already, like old Gorgonzola –

Moritz Please don't send me away.

Melchior Who are you, Sir?

Moritz Don't send me away, I beg you. Let me join in for a bit. I promise, whatever you say I shan't contradict you. But don't send me away yet. It's so freezingly horrible down there –

Masked Gentleman Not sublime? You told us it was sublime. Why do you go on with all that gaseous balderdash? Sour grapes! Rotten as well as sour. Why have you become such a liar – you miasma! But if you think you'll get any profit from our conversation, please do stay. Only keep your brainless fantasies to yourself. Perhaps inside that receptacle you're carrying. Stick your mouldy nose into your own business, by all means, but keep it out of mine.

Melchior Are you going to tell me who you are or not?

Masked Gentleman No. Here is my first piece of advice: trust me. Now – first priority: to get you away out of here.

Melchior Aren't you my father?

Masked Gentleman Wouldn't you recognize your father's voice?

Melchior No.

Masked Gentleman At this moment your father is consoling himself in the redoubtable arms of your mother. The secrets of this world are going to be opened for you. This despair you seem to be feeling is actually due to one thing only – your starved, exhausted condition. One hot meal will show you how to laugh at it.

Melchior This must be some devil. Unfortunately, my guilt is only too real. No hot meal is going to remove it.

Masked Gentleman Haha! That depends on the ingredients of the meal. Shall I tell you something? That girl would have had a perfect child. She was a near-perfect specimen herself. Then along comes Mother Schmidt's abortion technology – and there she is in the grave with her dead foetus. I will take you out into mankind. Opportunities that will fling your horizons wide in the most dazzling fashion. I will introduce you to every single thing of interest on this globe.

Melchior Who are you? I can't trust somebody I don't even know.

Masked Gentleman It's only by trusting me that you will find out who I am.

Melchior You're sure of that, are you?

Masked Gentleman Indeed I am. Anyway, you have no choice.

Melchior I can give my hand to my old friend here whenever I feel like it.

Masked Gentleman Your friend is a fraud. Nobody smiles who still has a penny in the bank. In this entire creation the most mournful object is the sublime comedian.

Melchior I care nothing about that. Either you tell me who you are or I give this comedian my hand.

Masked Gentleman Well?

Moritz Melchior, he's right. I was lying – I was bragging. Listen to him. Take him seriously. Ignore the mask. What he says is the truth. Let him show you a good time and use him. No matter how masked he may be, at least he wears one.

Melchior Do you believe in God?

Masked Gentleman Now that depends.

Melchior Who invented gunpowder?

Masked Gentleman Berthold Schwarz – also known as Konstantin Anklitzen – a Franciscan monk at Freiburg. He invented it in 1330.

Moritz Unfortunately.

Masked Gentleman You'd have hanged yourself.

Melchior What view do you take on morality?

Masked Gentleman Am I a schoolboy in your class?

Melchior I don't know what you are.

Moritz Whatever you do, don't quarrel, please. That won't help anything. What's the point of us sitting here together in a graveyard – two living bodies and one corpse – at half-past three in the morning, if all we're going to do is squabble like drunks. My share in this conversation was supposed to be a pleasure for me. If you're determined to quarrel, I'll just tuck my head back under my arm and go.

Melchior Still can't face the music.

Masked Gentleman The ghost is right. One's sense of dignity is also important: it must be kept up. Let me answer your question. Morality, as I understand it, is the real product of two imaginary forces. These two imaginary forces are duty and inclination. The real product is morality. Its existence is unarguable.

Moritz Why didn't somebody tell me that? My notion of morality killed me. On behalf of my parents, I shot myself. 'Honour thy father and mother that thy days may be long upon the earth.' The Bible wasn't thinking of me, was it? Oh, no, the Bible made a complete ass of itself over me!

Masked Gentleman Don't delude yourself, my friend. Your parents would never have died of your failure – any more than you needed to. They would have screamed and foamed for a while, to boil the hot air off – for the good of their health – nothing more.

Melchior I expect you're right. But, Sir, allow me to say, had I given my hand to Moritz just now, as I very nearly did, my sense of morality alone would have been responsible.

Masked Gentleman But because you are not Moritz – you didn't.

Moritz The difference between us isn't so great. It could have been me you bumped into that time I was dragging myself through the alder thickets with the pistol in my pocket.

Masked Gentleman Have I slipped from your memory so lightly? Those last moments of yours, when you too swayed between life and death – But I feel this is hardly the proper setting, if we're to prolong our intriguing little discussion.

Moritz It's getting very cold, gentlemen. They gave me my Sunday suit, but left off my shirt and underwear.

Melchior Farewell, dear Moritz. Who knows where this fellow will lead me. But at least he's a human being –

Moritz Don't hold it against me that I tried to get you over on to my side, Melchior. Old friendship dies hard. I'd happily groan and moan the rest of my life away if only I could come with you, out of this place.

Masked Gentleman In the end, everyone receives what they've earned. For you, the great peace of possessing nothing. And for you, the hopes of having everything to come – insatiable, overwhelming, doubtful.

Melchior Farewell, Moritz. Thank you for revealing yourself to me. Remember those fourteen years we were so close, and the happy times we had. No matter what happens to me, however these coming years alter me, whether things go well or badly with me, I promise you, Moritz, I shall not forget you –

Moritz Thank you, beloved friend.

Melchior And one day, when I'm old, with white hair, maybe once again you'll seem closer to me than anybody alive.

Moritz Goodbye, Melchior. Good luck go with you, gentlemen. Don't let me detain you any longer.

Masked Gentleman Come, my child.

The masked gentleman and Melchior go.

Moritz With my head under my arm, here I sit. Now the moon covers her face. And now she uncovers it. But still she has nothing to tell me. I must get back to my den. Straighten the cross that idiot blundered into so clumsily. Then when everything's neat and tidy, I'll stretch out on my back, let the putrefaction warm me up a bit, and I'll smile –